William Shakespeare's

All's Well That Ends Well

In Plain and Simple English

A SwipeSpeare™ Book
www.SwipeSpeare.com

Table of Contents

About This Series

The "SwipeSpeare™" series started as a way of telling Shakespeare for the modern reader—being careful to preserve the themes and integrity of the original. Visit our website SwipeSpeare.com to see other books in the series, as well as the interactive, and swipe-able, app!

The series is expanding every month. Visit BookCaps.com to see non-Shakespeare books in this series, and while you are there join the Facebook page, so you are first to know when a new book comes out.

Characters

KING OF FRANCE.

THE DUKE OF FLORENCE.BERTRAM, Count of Rousillon.

LAFEU, an old Lord.

PAROLLES, a follower of Bertram.

Several young French Lords, that serve with Bertram in theFlorentine War.

Steward, Servant to the Countess of Rousillon.

Clown, Servant to the Countess of Rousillon.

A Page, Servant to the Countess of Rousillon.

COUNTESS OF ROUSILLON, Mother to Bertram.

HELENA, a Gentlewoman protected by the Countess.

An old Widow of Florence.

DIANA, daughter to the Widow.

VIOLENTA, neighbour and friend to the Widow.

MARIANA, neighbour and friend to the Widow.

Lords attending on the KING; Officers; Soldiers, &c., French and Florentine.

Comparative Version

Act 1

SCENE I. Rousillon. The COUNT's palace.

Enter BERTRAM, the COUNTESS of Rousillon, HELENA, and LAFEU, all in black

COUNTESS
In delivering my son from me, I bury a second husband.

In sending away my son, it is as if I buried my husband again.

BERTRAM
And I in going, madam, weep o'er my father's death
anew: but I must attend his majesty's command, to
whom I am now in ward, evermore in subjection.

*And in going away, madam, I weep for my father's death
over again: but I must obey his Majesty's command,
for he is now my guardian and I am forever under his rule.*

LAFEU
You shall find of the king a husband, madam; you,
sir, a father: he that so generally is at all times
good must of necessity hold his virtue to you; whose
worthiness would stir it up where it wanted rather
than lack it where there is such abundance.

*You shall find the king like a husband, madam;
you
sir will find him like a father: he is always so good
that he will of course be good to you; you
deserve it and would provoke goodness if it was lacking,
so you will not lack it where there is so much available.*

COUNTESS
What hope is there of his majesty's amendment?

What hope is there of his Majesty getting better?

LAFEU
He hath abandoned his physicians, madam;
under whose
practises he hath persecuted time with hope, and
finds no other advantage in the process but only the
losing of hope by time.

*He has given up on his doctors, madam; he had
hoped to get more time through them, and now
he thinks that the only thing they can give him
is that he will lose hope over time.*

COUNTESS
This young gentlewoman had a father,--O, that
'had'! how sad a passage 'tis!--whose skill was
almost as great as his honesty; had it stretched so
far, would have made nature immortal, and death

*This young lady had a father–oh how sad
it is to say 'had'!–whose skill was almost as great
as his honesty; if it had been he could have made
mankind immortal, and death would have had*

should have play for lack of work. Would, for the
king's sake, he were living! I think it would be the death of the king's disease.

LAFEU
How called you the man you speak of, madam?

COUNTESS
He was famous, sir, in his profession, and it was his great right to be so: Gerard de Narbon.

LAFEU
He was excellent indeed, madam: the king very lately spoke of him admiringly and mourningly:
he
was skilful enough to have lived still, if knowledge
could be set up against mortality.

BERTRAM
What is it, my good lord, the king languishes of?

LAFEU
A fistula, my lord.

BERTRAM
I heard not of it before.

LAFEU
I would it were not notorious. Was this gentlewoman
the daughter of Gerard de Narbon?

COUNTESS
His sole child, my lord, and bequeathed to my overlooking. I have those hopes of her good that her education promises; her dispositions she inherits, which makes fair gifts fairer; for where an unclean mind carries virtuous qualities, there commendations go with pity; they are virtues and
traitors too; in her they are the better for their simpleness; she derives her honesty and achieves her goodness.

---

time on his hands through lack of work. I wish he were alive,
for the King's sake! I think he would have killed off the King's disease.

What was the name of this man you speak of, madam?

He was famous in his profession, Sir, and he had every right to be: Gerard de Narbon.

He was indeed a great man, madam: just recently
the King spoke of him admiringly and sadly: he had the skills to still be alive, if knowledge could triumph over death.

What is the nature of the King's illness, my good lord?

He has a fistula, my Lord.

I have never heard of that.

I wish nobody had. Was this young lady the daughter of Gerard de Narbon?

His only child, my lord, and left in my care. I have high hopes for her due to
the education she has received; she has inherited a good character which improves her gifts; when an unclean mind has good qualities, praise goes along with pity; they are virtues but
they are corrupted; in her they are better for her innocence; she inherits her honesty and has worked for her goodness.

LAFEU
Your commendations, madam, get from her
tears.

Your praise has made her cry, madam.

COUNTESS
'Tis the best brine a maiden can season her
praise
in. The remembrance of her father never
approaches
her heart but the tyranny of her sorrows takes all
livelihood from her cheek. No more of this,
Helena;
go to, no more; lest it be rather thought you
affect
a sorrow than have it.

*Tears give the best salt for a girl to flavour her
praise with.*
*She can never remember her father
without her great sorrow draining all the colour
from her cheeks.*
*Stop this, Helena; come on, stop it, you don't
want people to think
that your sorrow isn't genuine.*

HELENA
I do affect a sorrow indeed, but I have it too.

*I am making a show of mourning, but it is
genuine.*

LAFEU
Moderate lamentation is the right of the dead,
excessive grief the enemy to the living.

*The dead have a right to expect a little
mourning,
but excessive grief damages the living.*

COUNTESS
If the living be enemy to the grief, the excess
makes it soon mortal.

*If those who are alive fight against the grief,
it will soon die.*

BERTRAM
Madam, I desire your holy wishes.

Madam, I want your blessing.

LAFEU
How understand we that?

What does that mean?

COUNTESS
Be thou blest, Bertram, and succeed thy father
In manners, as in shape! thy blood and virtue
Contend for empire in thee, and thy goodness
Share with thy birthright! Love all, trust a few,
Do wrong to none: be able for thine enemy
Rather in power than use, and keep thy friend
Under thy own life's key: be cheque'd for
silence,
But never tax'd for speech. What heaven more
will,

*Bertram, may you have the blessing of copying
your father's
manners as well as his shape! Your passion and
your virtues
fight to rule over you, and your goodness
fights with your inheritance! Love everyone,
only trust a few,
do no harm to any; be prepared for your enemy
but don't attack him, and defend your friends
with your life: don't be too quiet,*

That thee may furnish and my prayers pluck down,
Fall on thy head! Farewell, my lord;
'Tis an unseason'd courtier; good my lord,
Advise him.

LAFEU
He cannot want the best
That shall attend his love.

Exit

BERTRAM
[To HELENA] The best wishes that can be forged in
your thoughts be servants to you! Be comfortable
to my mother, your mistress, and make much of her.

LAFEU
Farewell, pretty lady: you must hold the credit of
your father.

Oh, if that was it!

Exeunt BERTRAM and LAFEU

HELENA
O, were that all! I think not on my father;
And these great tears grace his remembrance more
Than those I shed for him. What was he like?
I have forgot him: my imagination
Carries no favour in't but Bertram's.
I am undone: there is no living, none,
If Bertram be away. 'Twere all one
That I should love a bright particular star
And think to wed it, he is so above me:
In his bright radiance and collateral light
Must I be comforted, not in his sphere.
The ambition in my love thus plagues itself:
The hind that would be mated by the lion
Must die for love. 'Twas pretty, though plague,
To see him every hour, to sit and draw
His arched brows, his hawking eye, his curls,

forgot

In our heart's table; heart too capable

his – BERTRAM
him – DAD

BERTRAM is A STAR!

hind – deer
(MATe) (MATing)

ARCh–ed

10

but don't talk too much. May whatever else
heaven will allow, and my prayers get for you,
fall upon your head! Farewell, my lord;
he is not used to courts; my good lord,
look after him.

He will get the best he deserves.

May your thoughts be full of goodness! Be good
to my mother, your mistress, and look after her.

(Arch-ed)

Goodbye, pretty lady: be a credit to your father.

Oh if that were all! I'm not thinking of my
father:
I am weeping more for the memory of him
than I am for his person. What was he like?
I have forgotten him: my mind
has no love in it except for Bertram.
I am lost: I cannot live at all
without Bertram. I might just as well
be in love with a bright star above
and think I could marry it, he is so far above
me:
I must be happy to bathe in his reflected light,
because I cannot get near to him.
And so my love tortures itself:
the deer that wanted to mate with a lion
would die of love. It was lovely, though torture,
to see him all the time, to sit and draw
a picture in my heart of his arched brows,

(drawing is
in my heart's
"table")

To see him every hour;
to sit And draw
his ARched brows, his hawking
eye, his curls,

In our heart's table|

heart too CAPAble

Of every line And trick of his
sweet favour:

Of every line and trick of his sweet favour:
But now he's gone, and my idolatrous fancy
Must sanctify his reliques. Who comes here?

Aside
One that goes with him: I love him for his sake;
And yet I know him a notorious liar,
Think him a great way fool, solely a coward;
Yet these fixed evils sit so fit in him,
That they take place, when virtue's steely bones
Look bleak i' the cold wind: withal, full oft we
see
Cold wisdom waiting on superfluous folly.

PAROLLES
Save you, fair queen!

HELENA
And you, monarch!

PAROLLES
No.

HELENA
And no.

PAROLLES
Are you meditating on virginity?

HELENA
Ay. You have some stain of soldier in you: let
me
ask you a question. Man is enemy to virginity;
how
may we barricado it against him?

PAROLLES
Keep him out.

HELENA
But he assails; and our virginity, though valiant,
in the defence yet is weak: unfold to us some
warlike resistance.

PAROLLES

---

*his sharp eye: my heart knows all too well
every little line of his sweet face:
but now he's gone, and all I have left to worship
are my memories of him. Who's this?*

*It's one of those that goes with him: I love him
for what he is,
and yet I know he is a terrible liar,
I think he is very foolish, a complete coward;
yet he is so suited to his flaws
that they look good, when cold virtues
look harsh: it's true that we often see
cold wisdom is not as attractive as foolishness.*

Greetings, lovely Queen!

The same to you, King!

I'm not a king.

And I'm not a Queen.

Are you thinking about virginity?

*Yes. You have something of the soldier about
you: let me
ask you a question. Man is the enemy of
virginity; how
can we resist him?*

Keep him out.

*But he attacks, and although our virginity is
brave,
it is weak in its defence: tell me a soldier's way
of resisting.*

There is none: man, sitting down before you, will
undermine you and blow you up.

HELENA

Bless our poor virginity from underminers and blowers up! Is there no military policy, how virgins might blow up men?

PAROLLES

Virginity being blown down, man will quicklier be
blown up: marry, in blowing him down again, with
the breach yourselves made, you lose your city. It
is not politic in the commonwealth of nature to preserve virginity. Loss of virginity is rational increase and there was never virgin got till virginity was first lost. That you were made of is metal to make virgins. Virginity by being once lost
may be ten times found; by being ever kept, it is ever lost: 'tis too cold a companion; away with 't!

HELENA

I will stand for 't a little, though therefore I die a virgin.

PAROLLES

There's little can be said in 't; 'tis against the rule of nature. To speak on the part of virginity, is to accuse your mothers; which is most infallible
disobedience. He that hangs himself is a virgin: virginity murders itself and should be buried in highways out of all sanctified limit, as a desperate
offendress against nature. Virginity breeds mites,
much like a cheese; consumes itself to the very paring, and so dies with feeding his own stomach.
Besides, virginity is peevish, proud, idle, made of

There isn't one: a man, sitting down in front of you, will
get under your defences and blow you up.

Save our poor virginity from these underminers and blowers up! Is there no military way for virgins to blow up men?

Once virginity has been beaten, men will quickly be blown up: in fact, the action of blowing him down
will bring your city walls tumbling. It's not part of nature
to preserve virginity. The loss of virginity means the increase
of the population, no virgin was ever born unless
somebody lost their virginity first. You were made
to make virgins. Once your virginity is lost you can make ten more virgins; if you keep it there will be no more virgins: it's a cold companion, get rid of it!

I think I'll put up with it for a while, even if it means I died a virgin.

There's not much to be said for it; it's against the law of nature. If you defend virginity then you are attacking your mother; which is a terrible
thing to do. A suicide is a virgin: virginity murders itself and should be buried by the roadside, not in the holy ground, as being a terrible
offender against nature. Virginity breeds parasites
like a cheese does; it eats itself right down to the rind, and so dies feeding
itself.
Besides, virginity is testy, arrogant, lazy, made of

self-love, which is the most inhibited sin in the canon. Keep it not; you cannot choose but loose by't: out with 't! within ten year it will make itself ten, which is a goodly increase; and the principal itself not much the worse: away with 't!

HELENA
How might one do, sir, to lose it to her own liking?

PAROLLES
Let me see: marry, ill, to like him that ne'er it likes. 'Tis a commodity will lose the gloss with lying; the longer kept, the less worth: off with 't while 'tis vendible; answer the time of request. Virginity, like an old courtier, wears her cap out of fashion: richly suited, but unsuitable: just like the brooch and the tooth-pick, which wear not now. Your date is better in your pie and your porridge than in your cheek; and your virginity, your old virginity, is like one of our French withered pears, it looks ill, it eats drily; marry, 'tis a withered pear; it was formerly better; marry, yet 'tis a withered pear: will you anything with it?

HELENA
Not my virginity yet
There shall your master have a thousand loves,
A mother and a mistress and a friend,
A phoenix, captain and an enemy,
A guide, a goddess, and a sovereign,
A counsellor, a traitress, and a dear;
His humble ambition, proud humility,
His jarring concord, and his discord dulcet,
His faith, his sweet disaster; with a world
Of pretty, fond, adoptious christendoms,
That blinking Cupid gossips. Now shall he--
I know not what he shall. God send him well!
The court's a learning place, and he is one—

PAROLLES
What one, i' faith?

---

self-love, which is the most prohibited sin of all. Don't hang onto it, you will only lose by doing so: get rid of it! Within ten years you will have made ten more virgins, which is a good return; and you won't have lost much of your capital. Get rid of it!

What should one do, Sir, to lose it in a pleasing manner?

Let me see; well, you must like someone who doesn't like virginity; it's a commodity that will go off; the longer you keep it, the less it is worth: get rid of it while it's still saleable; give it up when asked. Virginity, like an old courtier, wears an unfashionable cap: good quality, but unsuitable: like brooches and toothpicks, which nobody wears now. Dates are nicer in pies or in porridge than eaten raw; and your virginity, your old virginity, is like one of those dried French pears, it looks nasty, it's dry to eat; in fact it's a withered pear: what can you do with it?

*Your master shall not have my virginity yet, but he will have thousand loves,
a mother and a mistress and friend,
a phoenix, a captain and an enemy,
a guide, a Goddess and Queen,
a counsellor, a traitoress and a dear one;
his humble ambition, his proud humility,
his clashing harmonies, his sweet discord,
his faith, his sweet disaster; these are all
the pretty, fond, adopted names
that men give, inspired by love. Now he shall–
I don't know what he shall. May God look after him! The court's a place where one learns, and he is one–*

For heaven's sake, who are you talking about?

14

HELENA
That I wish well. 'Tis pity—

The one that I wish well. It's a shame-

PAROLLES
What's pity?

What's a shame?

HELENA
That wishing well had not a body in't,
Which might be felt; that we, the poorer born,
Whose baser stars do shut us up in wishes,
Might with effects of them follow our friends,
And show what we alone must think, which never
Return us thanks.

*That good wishes don't have a physical body,
so that we who are born poor, whose lowly
position means wishes are all we have,
might use them to follow our friends,
and show them things we are only allowed to think,
which never do us any good.*

Enter Page

Page
Monsieur Parolles, my lord calls for you.

Monsieur Parolles, my lord wants you.

Exit

PAROLLES
Little Helen, farewell; if I can remember thee, I will think of thee at court.

Farewell little Helen; if I remember you, I will think of you when I'm at the court.

HELENA
Monsieur Parolles, you were born under a charitable star.

Monsieur Parolles, you were born under a star sign which makes you kind.

PAROLLES
Under Mars, I.

I was born under Mars.

HELENA
I especially think, under Mars.

Definitely under Mars, I think.

PAROLLES
Why under Mars?

Why under Mars?

HELENA
The wars have so kept you under that you must needs
be born under Mars.

*You can have been so much in the wars that you must
have been born under Mars.*

PAROLLES
When he was predominant.

When he was in the ascendant.

HELENA

When he was retrograde, I think, rather.

I think when he was descending, actually.

PAROLLES

Why think you so?

Why do you think that?

HELENA

You go so much backward when you fight.

You are always going backwards when you fight.

PAROLLES

That's for advantage.

That's to get an advantage.

HELENA

So is running away, when fear proposes the
safety;
but the composition that your valour and fear
makes
in you is a virtue of a good wing, and I like the
wear well.

*So is running away, when you're inspired by
fear;
but the mixture of your bravery and fear
makes a good outfit, and I like the look of it.*

PAROLLES

I am so full of businesses, I cannot answer thee
acutely. I will return perfect courtier; in the
which, my instruction shall serve to naturalize
thee, so thou wilt be capable of a courtier's
counsel and understand what advice shall thrust
upon
thee; else thou diest in thine unthankfulness, and
thine ignorance makes thee away: farewell.
When
thou hast leisure, say thy prayers; when thou
hast
none, remember thy friends; get thee a good
husband,
and use him as he uses thee; so, farewell.

*I'm too busy to answer you properly.
I will come back the perfect courtier; and when
I do
I will teach you all the ways of the court
so you will be ready for a courtier's
advice and be able to understand it;
otherwise you'll die lonely,
kept alone by your ignorance: goodbye.
When you have the time, say your prayers;
don't bother remembering your friends;
get yourself a husband and
treat him the same as he treats you.*

Exit

HELENA

Our remedies oft in ourselves do lie,
Which we ascribe to heaven: the fated sky
Gives us free scope, only doth backward pull
Our slow designs when we ourselves are dull.
What power is it which mounts my love so high,
That makes me see, and cannot feed mine eye?

*We have the power to take fate into our own
hands, which we usually say is controlled by the
stars; the fateful sky gives us free rein, it only
our clumsy plans when we are clumsy ourselves.
What is the power that gives me so much love,
that lets me look when I cannot touch?*

The mightiest space in fortune nature brings
To join like likes and kiss like native things.
Impossible be strange attempts to those
That weigh their pains in sense and do suppose
What hath been cannot be: who ever strove
So show her merit, that did miss her love?
The king's disease--my project may deceive me,
But my intents are fix'd and will not leave me.

Exit

Fate leaves a space for nature to come in,
to join those who are similar and let them
naturally kiss. Strange plans look impossible to
those who weigh things in the balance sensibly
and think that nothing can be changed: who was
there who ever
showed such merit, missing her love?
The king's disease-I may be deceiving myself
with this plan,
but my mind is made up, I'm going ahead.

SCENE II. Paris. The KING's palace.

Flourish of cornets. Enter the KING of France, with letters, and divers Attendants

KING
The Florentines and Senoys are by the ears;
Have fought with equal fortune and continue
A braving war.

The Florentines and the Siennese are still at loggerheads; they have had equal success and are continuing a fierce war.

First Lord
So 'tis reported, sir.

So they say, sir.

KING
Nay, 'tis most credible; we here received it
A certainty, vouch'd from our cousin Austria,
With caution that the Florentine will move us
For speedy aid; wherein our dearest friend
Prejudicates the business and would seem
To have us make denial.

No, you can believe it; I've been told it's definite by my cousin the King of Austria, who warns that the Florentines will be coming to us looking for help; and our dear friend has weighed up the matter and seems to want us to refuse.

First Lord
His love and wisdom,
Approved so to your majesty, may plead
For amplest credence.

His love and wisdom, which your Majesty so values, means we should give his views the greatest respect.

KING
He hath arm'd our answer,
And Florence is denied before he comes:
Yet, for our gentlemen that mean to see
The Tuscan service, freely have they leave
To stand on either part.

He has prepared our answer for us, and Florence is refused before she asks. But for any of our gentlemen who want to fight in Tuscany, they have my permission to fight for either side.

Second Lord
It well may serve
A nursery to our gentry, who are sick
For breathing and exploit.

It may well be a good training ground for our gentry, who are itching for exercise and adventure.

KING
What's he comes here?

Who's this coming?

Enter BERTRAM, LAFEU, and PAROLLES

First Lord
It is the Count Rousillon, my good lord,

It is Count Rousillon, my good lord,

Young Bertram.

KING
Youth, thou bear'st thy father's face;
Frank nature, rather curious than in haste,
Hath well composed thee. Thy father's moral parts
Mayst thou inherit too! Welcome to Paris.

BERTRAM
My thanks and duty are your majesty's.

KING
I would I had that corporal soundness now,
As when thy father and myself in friendship
First tried our soldiership! He did look far
Into the service of the time and was
Disciped of the bravest: he lasted long;
But on us both did haggish age steal on
And wore us out of act. It much repairs me
To talk of your good father. In his youth
He had the wit which I can well observe
To-day in our young lords; but they may jest
Till their own scorn return to them unnoted
Ere they can hide their levity in honour;
So like a courtier, contempt nor bitterness
Were in his pride or sharpness; if they were,
His equal had awaked them, and his honour,
Clock to itself, knew the true minute when
Exception bid him speak, and at this time
His tongue obey'd his hand: who were below him
He used as creatures of another place
And bow'd his eminent top to their low ranks,
Making them proud of his humility,
In their poor praise he humbled. Such a man
Might be a copy to these younger times;
Which, follow'd well, would demonstrate them now
But goers backward.

BERTRAM
His good remembrance, sir,
Lies richer in your thoughts than on his tomb;
So in approof lives not his epitaph
As in your royal speech.

young Bertram.

Young man, you look like your father;
nature has clearly worked carefully, not swiftly,
and made you well. May you also have inherited
your father's moral character! Welcome to Paris.

I give you my thanks, and I am at your Majesty's service.

I wish that I was as healthy now
as I was when your father and I in friendship
First became soldiers! He spent a long time in
service and had the bravest followers: he lasted
for a long time; but that old witch, age, crept up
on us and curtailed our actions. It cheers me up
to talk about your good father. In his youth
he was as witty as the young lords
whom I see today; but they can joke
until they're blue in the face before they can
match their wit with honour;
he was so courteous, there was no contempt or bitterness
in his pride or his wit; if there was
it was only ever to his equals, and his honour,
which governed him, knew the right time
to speak when he was offended, and at this time
his tongue would follow his hand: those below him
he treated as if they had a different position
and bowed his noble head to their lower ranks,
making them delighted with his humility; he
humbled himself to praise them. A man like this
would be a good example for modern times;
if it was followed, it would show these young ones
that they have actually fallen backwards.

The best memorial for him, Sir,
is your memories rather than what's written on
his tomb; your royal speech is the best
confirmation of his epitaph.

KING

Would I were with him! He would always say--
Methinks I hear him now; his plausive words
He scatter'd not in ears, but grafted them,
To grow there and to bear,--'Let me not live,'--
This his good melancholy oft began,
On the catastrophe and heel of pastime,
When it was out,--'Let me not live,' quoth he,
'After my flame lacks oil, to be the snuff
Of younger spirits, whose apprehensive senses
All but new things disdain; whose judgments are
Mere fathers of their garments; whose constancies
Expire before their fashions.' This he wish'd;
I after him do after him wish too,
Since I nor wax nor honey can bring home,
I quickly were dissolved from my hive,
To give some labourers room.

Second Lord

You are loved, sir:
They that least lend it you shall lack you first.

KING

I fill a place, I know't. How long is't, count,
Since the physician at your father's died?
He was much famed.

BERTRAM

Some six months since, my lord.

KING

If he were living, I would try him yet.
Lend me an arm; the rest have worn me out
With several applications; nature and sickness
Debate it at their leisure. Welcome, count;
My son's no dearer.

BERTRAM

Thank your majesty.

Exeunt. Flourish

*I wish I was with him! He would always say-
it's almost as if I can hear him now; he didn't
throw about his sensible words but planted them
to grow and bear fruit– 'let me not live,' -
that is how his sweet complaints often began,
when we got towards the end of some pastime or
when it was over- 'let me not live,' he would say,
'when my fire has no more fuel, to be a
dampener on younger spirits, whose senses
have contempt for everything but the new; their
wisdom is all spent thinking of their clothes;
their loyalties
don't last as long as their fashions.' This is what
he wished; and I wish the same as him,
since I cannot bring home wax or honey
I should be quickly thrown out of my hive
to give the workers some room.*

*You are loved, sir;
even those who don't show it would be first to
miss you.*

*I'm taking up room, I know it. How long is it,
count, since your father's physician died?
He was very well-known.*

Six months ago, my lord.

*If he were alive I would give him a try.
Give me your arm; the others have worn me out
with their different medicines; nature and
sickness are fighting it out as they please.
Welcome, Count; you are as dear to me as my
son.*

Thank you, your Majesty.

SCENE III. Rousillon. The COUNT's palace.

Enter COUNTESS, Steward, and Clown

COUNTESS
I will now hear; what say you of this
gentlewoman?

*I'll listen to you now; what have you to say
about this gentlewoman?*

Steward
Madam, the care I have had to even your
content, I
wish might be found in the calendar of my past
endeavours; for then we wound our modesty and
make
foul the clearness of our deservings, when of
ourselves we publish them.

*Madam, the care I have taken over your
happiness I
hope can be seen in the records of the things I
have done
in the past; it is immodest, and makes us less
deserving,
to boast of our good deeds ourselves.*

COUNTESS
What does this knave here? Get you gone,
sirrah:
the complaints I have heard of you I do not all
believe: 'tis my slowness that I do not; for I
know
you lack not folly to commit them, and have
ability
enough to make such knaveries yours.

*What is this scoundrel doing here? Get out, sir:
I don't believe all the bad things I've heard
about you: it's stupid of me not to, for I know
that you are daft enough to do them, and have
the ability
to get up to that sort of mischief.*

Clown
'Tis not unknown to you, madam, I am a poor
fellow.

You know, madam, that I am a poor fellow.

COUNTESS
Well, sir.

Well?

Clown
No, madam, 'tis not so well that I am poor,
though
many of the rich are damned: but, if I may have
your ladyship's good will to go to the world,
Isbel
the woman and I will do as we may.

*No, madam, I don't think it's well that I am poor,
although
many of the rich will go to hell: but, if I can
have your ladyship's kind permission to go out
into the world, the woman Isbel and I will get
by as best we can.*

COUNTESS
Wilt thou needs be a beggar?

Will you have to beg?

Clown

I do beg your good will in this case.

I'm begging for your blessing in this case.

COUNTESS

In what case?

In what case?

Clown

In Isbel's case and mine own. Service is no heritage: and I think I shall never have the blessing of God till I have issue o' my body; for they say barnes are blessings.

In Isbel's case and my own. Being a servant leaves nothing: and I think I will never have the blessing of God until I have children; for they say babies are blessings.

COUNTESS

Tell me thy reason why thou wilt marry.

Tell me why you want to get married.

Clown

My poor body, madam, requires it: I am driven on
by the flesh; and he must needs go that the devil drives.

My poor body, madam, demands it: I am driven by lust; when the devil orders one must obey.

COUNTESS

Is this all your worship's reason?

And this is your only reason?

Clown

Faith, madam, I have other holy reasons such as they are.

Oh no madam, I have other, holy, reasons; such as they are.

COUNTESS

May the world know them?

Can you tell us?

Clown

I have been, madam, a wicked creature, as you and
all flesh and blood are; and, indeed, I do marry that I may repent.

*Madam, I have been a wicked creature, just like you
and all humans; and so I am marrying
so that I can repent.*

COUNTESS

Thy marriage, sooner than thy wickedness.

You will regret your marriage before you regret your wickedness.

Clown

I am out o' friends, madam; and I hope to have friends for my wife's sake.

*I have no friends, madam; I hope people will come
to see me because of my wife.*

COUNTESS

Such friends are thine enemies, knave.

Friends like that are your enemies, fool.

Clown

You're shallow, madam, in great friends; for the knaves come to do that for me which I am aweary of.
He that ears my land spares my team and gives me
leave to in the crop; if I be his cuckold, he's my drudge: he that comforts my wife is the cherisher
of my flesh and blood; he that cherishes my flesh
and blood loves my flesh and blood; he that loves my
flesh and blood is my friend: ergo, he that kisses my wife is my friend. If men could be contented to
be what they are, there were no fear in marriage; for young Charbon the Puritan and old Poysam the
Papist, howsome'er their hearts are severed in religion, their heads are both one; they may jowl horns together, like any deer i' the herd.

You don't understand, madam, what great friends they are; the scoundrels come and do for me the things I am tired of.
Someone who ploughs my land gives my horses a rest and I can still gather the crop; if he's cheating on me, he's my dogsbody: the one who sleeps with my wife cares for my flesh and blood; anyone who cares for my flesh and blood loves my flesh and blood; anyone who loves my flesh and blood is my friend: therefore whoever kisses my wife is my friend. If men would be happy to be honest about who they are, there would be no anxiety in marriage; young Charbon the puritan and old Poysam the papist, however much their hearts are separated by religion, their minds are the same; they can lock horns with each other like any other deer in the herd.

COUNTESS

Wilt thou ever be a foul-mouthed and calumnious knave?

Will you always be a foulmouthed and slandering scoundrel?

Clown

A prophet I, madam; and I speak the truth the next
way:
For I the ballad will repeat,
Which men full true shall find;
Your marriage comes by destiny,
Your cuckoo sings by kind.

I am a prophet, madam; and I'm telling the truth in my way;
I will repeat the song which men will know is true; your marriage comes through fate, cheating comes through nature.

COUNTESS

Get you gone, sir; I'll talk with you more anon.

Away with you, sir; I'll talk to you more soon.

Steward

May it please you, madam, that he bid Helen come to
you: of her I am to speak.

If it's all right with you madam, ask him to tell Helen to come here; I need to speak to you about her.

COUNTESS

Sirrah, tell my gentlewoman I would speak with
her;
Helen, I mean.

*Sir, tell my gentlewoman that I want a word with
her;
Helen, I mean.*

Clown

Was this fair face the cause, quoth she,
Why the Grecians sacked Troy?
Fond done, done fond,
Was this King Priam's joy?
With that she sighed as she stood,
With that she sighed as she stood,
And gave this sentence then;
Among nine bad if one be good,
Among nine bad if one be good,
There's yet one good in ten.

*Was this fair face the reason, she asked,
for the Greeks sacking Troy?
It was done for love, for love,
was this King Priam's delight?
With that she sighed as she stood there,
with that she sighed as she stood there,
and she spoke this sentence;
if there are nine bad people and one good,
if there are nine bad people and one good,
that means there's still one good person in ten.*

COUNTESS

What, one good in ten? you corrupt the song,
sirrah.

One good in ten? You're twisting the song, Sir.

Clown

One good woman in ten, madam; which is a
purifying
o' the song: would God would serve the world
so all
the year! we'ld find no fault with the tithe-
woman,
if I were the parson. One in ten, quoth a'! An we
might have a good woman born but one every
blazing
star, or at an earthquake, 'twould mend the
lottery
well: a man may draw his heart out, ere a' pluck
one.

*One good woman in ten, madam; which cleans
up
the song: if only God could give us that
proportion!
If I were the parson I'd be quite happy with
a tenth of womankind. One in ten you say! If we
just had a good woman born for every shooting
start, or when there is an earthquake, it would
improve the odds: a man could tear out his
heart before he gets a good one.*

COUNTESS

You'll be gone, sir knave, and do as I command
you.

*You'll get out, you scoundrel, and do as you've
been told.*

Clown

That man should be at woman's command, and
yet no
hurt done! Though honesty be no puritan, yet it
will do no hurt; it will wear the surplice of

*That a man should be at a woman's command,
and yet
there's no harm done! Honesty is not a puritan,
but it won't do any harm; it will wear the*

24

humility over the black gown of a big heart. I am
going, forsooth: the business is for Helen to come hither.

Exit

COUNTESS
Well, now.

Steward
I know, madam, you love your gentlewoman entirely.

COUNTESS
Faith, I do: her father bequeathed her to me; and
she herself, without other advantage, may lawfully
make title to as much love as she finds: there is
more owing her than is paid; and more shall be paid
her than she'll demand.

Steward
Madam, I was very late more near her than I think
she wished me: alone she was, and did communicate
to herself her own words to her own ears; she
thought, I dare vow for her, they touched not any
stranger sense. Her matter was, she loved your son:
Fortune, she said, was no goddess, that had put
such difference betwixt their two estates; Love no
god, that would not extend his might, only where
qualities were level; Dian no queen of virgins, that
would suffer her poor knight surprised, without
rescue in the first assault or ransom afterward.
This she delivered in the most bitter touch of
sorrow that e'er I heard virgin exclaim in: which I
held my duty speedily to acquaint you withal;

surplice
of humility over the black gown of a big heart.
Alright,
I'm going! You want Helen to come here.

Right then.

I know, madam, that you completely love your
gentlewoman.

Indeed I do: her father left her to me; and she,
having been left nothing else, has a lawful claim
to as much love as she can get; she is owed
more than she is paid; and she will be paid
more than she will ask for.

Madam, I was recently closer to her than I think
she would have liked: she was alone and
was talking to herself; I am sure
she didn't know anyone else heard her words.
What she was saying was that she loved your
son:
she said that Fortune was no goddess, to have made
them both in such different classes; Love was
no god if he would only apply his force when
people were equal; Diana was no queen of virgins,
this she would allow her poor knight to be surprised,
if he couldn't be rescued in the first attack or
ransomed afterwards.
She said all this in the most bitter and sorrowful
manner that I ever heard from a girl: so I thought
that it was my duty to let you know about it as
soon as possible;

sithence, in the loss that may happen, it concerns you something to know it.

seeing as what you could lose, it's your business to know what's going on.

COUNTESS
You have discharged this honestly; keep it to yourself: many likelihoods informed me of this before, which hung so tottering in the balance that
I could neither believe nor misdoubt. Pray you, leave me: stall this in your bosom; and I thank you
for your honest care: I will speak with you further anon.

You have done your duty well; keep it to yourself: there were many things before which made me
suspect this, but it was so finely balanced that I could neither believe nor disbelieve. Please, leave me: keep this yourself; and I thank you for your good service: I'll speak more to you soon.

Exit Steward

Enter HELENA
Even so it was with me when I was young:
If ever we are nature's, these are ours; this thorn
Doth to our rose of youth rightly belong;
Our blood to us, this to our blood is born;
It is the show and seal of nature's truth,
Where love's strong passion is impress'd in youth:
By our remembrances of days foregone,
Such were our faults, or then we thought them none.
Her eye is sick on't: I observe her now.

It was just like this with me when I was young: this comes from our natures; this thorn is a proper part of the rose of our youth; it is as much a part of it as our blood; it is symbolic of the force of nature, where the passion of love is embedded in the young:
I can remember the days gone by, when I had these faults, although we didn't think they were faults then.
She is sick with it: I can see her now.

HELENA
What is your pleasure, madam?

What would you like me to do, madam?

COUNTESS
You know, Helen,
I am a mother to you.

You know, Helen,
that I am a mother to you.

HELENA
Mine honourable mistress.

My honourable mistress.

COUNTESS
Nay, a mother:
Why not a mother? When I said 'a mother,'
Methought you saw a serpent: what's in 'mother,'
That you start at it? I say, I am your mother;
And put you in the catalogue of those

No, a mother:
why not a mother? When I said 'a mother,' you looked as though you'd seen a snake: what is it about 'mother,'
that makes you shy away? I tell you, I am your

That were enwombed mine: 'tis often seen
Adoption strives with nature and choice breeds
A native slip to us from foreign seeds:
You ne'er oppress'd me with a mother's groan,
Yet I express to you a mother's care:
God's mercy, maiden! does it curd thy blood
To say I am thy mother? What's the matter,
That this distemper'd messenger of wet,
The many-colour'd Iris, rounds thine eye?
Why? that you are my daughter?

HELENA
That I am not.

COUNTESS
I say, I am your mother.

HELENA
Pardon, madam;
The Count Rousillon cannot be my brother:
I am from humble, he from honour'd name;
No note upon my parents, his all noble:
My master, my dear lord he is; and I
His servant live, and will his vassal die:
He must not be my brother.

COUNTESS
Nor I your mother?

HELENA
You are my mother, madam; would you were,--
So that my lord your son were not my brother,--
Indeed my mother! or were you both our
mothers,
I care no more for than I do for heaven,
So I were not his sister. Can't no other,
But, I your daughter, he must be my brother?

COUNTESS
Yes, Helen, you might be my daughter-in-law:
God shield you mean it not! daughter and
mother
So strive upon your pulse. What, pale again?
My fear hath catch'd your fondness: now I see
The mystery of your loneliness, and find
Your salt tears' head: now to all sense 'tis gross

mother;
I include you in the list of the ones
that came from my womb: it is often the case
that adoption fights with nature and breeding
and things from foreign seeds become native.
I never had the pain of giving birth to you,
but I offer you the care of a mother: good God,
girl! Would it kill you to say I am your mother?
Why are these tears falling from your eyes?
Is it because you are my daughter?

I am not your daughter.

I'm telling you I am your mother.

Excuse me, madam;
Count Rousillon cannot be my brother.
I come from a humble background, him from a
noble one; my parents had no fame, his are all
noble: he is my master, my dear lord; and I
live as his servant, and will die the same:
he cannot be my brother.

So I can't be your mother?

You are my mother, madam; but I wish it was-
that my Lord your son was not my brother-
you are my mother indeed! Or if you were
mother to us both,
I would give up heaven to not be his sister. Can't
it be any other way than that
being your daughter, he must be my brother?

Yes Helen, you could be my daughter-in-law.
I hope to God you don't mean it! Daughter and
mother
seem to be words that upset you. What, you've
gone pale again? My fears have revealed newer
affections: now I see more you have been lonely,
and why the tears have been flowing: now it's

You love my son; invention is ashamed,
Against the proclamation of thy passion,
To say thou dost not: therefore tell me true;
But tell me then, 'tis so; for, look thy cheeks
Confess it, th' one to th' other; and thine eyes
See it so grossly shown in thy behaviors
That in their kind they speak it: only sin
And hellish obstinacy tie thy tongue,
That truth should be suspected. Speak, is't so?
If it be so, you have wound a goodly clew;
If it be not, forswear't: howe'er, I charge thee,
As heaven shall work in me for thine avail,
Tell me truly.

HELENA
Good madam, pardon me!

COUNTESS
Do you love my son?

HELENA
Your pardon, noble mistress!

COUNTESS
Love you my son?

HELENA
Do not you love him, madam?

COUNTESS
Go not about; my love hath in't a bond,
Whereof the world takes note: come, come,
disclose
The state of your affection; for your passions
Have to the full appeach'd.

HELENA
Then, I confess,
Here on my knee, before high heaven and you,
That before you, and next unto high heaven,
I love your son.
My friends were poor, but honest; so's my love:
Be not offended; for it hurts not him
That he is loved of me: I follow him not
By any token of presumptuous suit;

---

perfectly obvious
that you love my son; there are no lying excuses
which can cover up your passion
and say it's not true: so tell me the truth;
just tell me, you know it's the truth; your blushes
give you away. Your eyes
show it so obviously it's as if they are talking:
only sin and hell are making you keep your
obstinate silence, to try and cover up the truth.
Speak, is this the case? If it is so, you have
weaved a tangled web; if it is not, swear to it:
whichever way, I order you, as heaven shall
help me to help you, tell me the truth.

Good madam, forgive me!

Do you love my son?

Noble mistress, please forgive me!

Do you love my son?

Don't you love him, madam?

Don't change the subject; my love has a reason
for it
acknowledged by society: come on, admit
to your feelings; for your passions
have given you away.

Then I admit,
here on my knees, before you and heaven,
that more than you, and equal to heaven,
I love your son.
My relatives were poor, but honest; and so is my
love: do not be cross; it does not hurt him
to be loved by me: I am not chasing after him
with impertinent demands;

Nor would I have him till I do deserve him;
Yet never know how that desert should be.
I know I love in vain, strive against hope;
Yet in this captious and intenible sieve
I still pour in the waters of my love
And lack not to lose still: thus, Indian-like,
Religious in mine error, I adore
The sun, that looks upon his worshipper,
But knows of him no more. My dearest madam,
Let not your hate encounter with my love
For loving where you do: but if yourself,
Whose aged honour cites a virtuous youth,
Did ever in so true a flame of liking
Wish chastely and love dearly, that your Dian
Was both herself and love: O, then, give pity
To her, whose state is such that cannot choose
But lend and give where she is sure to lose;
That seeks not to find that her search implies,
But riddle-like lives sweetly where she dies!

COUNTESS
Had you not lately an intent,--speak truly,--
To go to Paris?

HELENA
Madam, I had.

COUNTESS
Wherefore? tell true.

HELENA
I will tell truth; by grace itself I swear.
You know my father left me some prescriptions
Of rare and proved effects, such as his reading
And manifest experience had collected
For general sovereignty; and that he will'd me
In heedfull'st reservation to bestow them,
As notes whose faculties inclusive were
More than they were in note: amongst the rest,
There is a remedy, approved, set down,
To cure the desperate languishings whereof
The king is render'd lost.

COUNTESS
This was your motive
For Paris, was it? speak.

*nor would I have him until I deserve him, and
I do not know what I can do to deserve him.
I know that I love in vain, that it's probably
hopeless; but I still pour the water of my love
into this huge and leaky sieve
and still have plenty more to give: so, like an
Indian following a wrong religion, I worship
the sun, that looks down on his worshipper
but does not see him. My dearest madam,
do not hate me just because I love
the same one you do: if you yourself,
whose respect in age shows you had a virtuous
youth, ever felt such a true love that you
retained your chastity despite the fact that your
love was burning you up inside? oh then give
pity, to her whose position is such that all she
can do please give her love where it is sure to be
lost; she does not think that she will get the
thing she is looking for, but paradoxically feels
she's winning when she's losing.*

*Weren't you recently planning-tell the truth-
to go to Paris?*

Madam, I was.

Why? Tell the truth.

*I will tell the truth; I swear by heaven.
You know my father left me some recipes for
medicine of great and proven worth, that he had
collected through his reading and great
experience for the good of all; and he ordered
me
To keep them carefully tucked away,
as they were more effective than they were well
known. Amongst the rest there is a proven
remedy written down which can cure the terrible
illness which has attacked the King.*

*And that was why you wanted
to go to Paris, was it? Out with it.*

HELENA
My lord your son made me to think of this;
Else Paris and the medicine and the king
Had from the conversation of my thoughts
Haply been absent then.

My lord your son set me thinking of this;
otherwise Paris and the medicine and the King
would never have entered into my thoughts.

COUNTESS
But think you, Helen,
If you should tender your supposed aid,
He would receive it? he and his physicians
Are of a mind; he, that they cannot help him,
They, that they cannot help: how shall they credit
A poor unlearned virgin, when the schools,
Embowell'd of their doctrine, have left off
The danger to itself?

But do you think, Helen,
that if you offer him your help
he would accept it? He and his physicians
think the same thing; he thinks that they cannot
help him, they think that they cannot help: what
credence will they give
to a poor uneducated virgin, when all the
educated have run out of ideas and left the
illness to run its course?

HELENA
There's something in't,
More than my father's skill, which was the greatest
Of his profession, that his good receipt
Shall for my legacy be sanctified
By the luckiest stars in heaven: and, would your honour
But give me leave to try success, I'ld venture
The well-lost life of mine on his grace's cure
By such a day and hour.

There's something more in it
than my father's skill (and he was the greatest
of his profession) that means
this recipe he has given me will be blessed
by the luckiest stars in heaven: and if your honor
would just give me permission to try it I'll bet
my life on his Grace being cured
by a specific time I set.

COUNTESS
Dost thou believe't?

And you believe this is true?

HELENA
Ay, madam, knowingly.

Yes madam, I know it is.

COUNTESS
Why, Helen, thou shalt have my leave and love,
Means and attendants and my loving greetings
To those of mine in court: I'll stay at home
And pray God's blessing into thy attempt:
Be gone to-morrow; and be sure of this,
What I can help thee to thou shalt not miss.

Why then, Helen, you have my permission and
my love, you shall have money, servants, and
take my loving greetings
to my relatives in the court: I'll stay at home
and pray that God blesses your efforts:
go tomorrow; and I can promise you
I'll leave no stone unturned to help you.

Exeunt

Act 2

SCENE I. Paris. The KING's palace.

Flourish of cornets. Enter the KING, attended with divers young Lords taking leave for the Florentine war; BERTRAM, and PAROLLES

KING

Farewell, young lords; these warlike principles
Do not throw from you: and you, my lords,
farewell:
Share the advice betwixt you; if both gain, all
The gift doth stretch itself as 'tis received,
And is enough for both.

*Farewell, young lords; do not forget
these principles of war: and farewell to you, my
lords :
share the advice amongst you; if you both take it
the gift will stretch and make enough for both of
you.*

First Lord

'Tis our hope, sir,
After well enter'd soldiers, to return
And find your grace in health.

*We hope, Sir,
that once we have acquitted ourselves well as
soldiers
we will come back to find your Grace recovered.*

KING

No, no, it cannot be; and yet my heart
Will not confess he owes the malady
That doth my life besiege. Farewell, young
lords;
Whether I live or die, be you the sons
Of worthy Frenchmen: let higher Italy,--
Those bated that inherit but the fall
Of the last monarchy,--see that you come
Not to woo honour, but to wed it; when
The bravest questant shrinks, find what you
seek,
That fame may cry you loud: I say, farewell.

*No, that will not happen; although my heart
won't admit to the seriousness of the illness
that is attacking my life. Farewell, young lords;
whether I live or die, acquit yourselves
as good Frenchmen: let great Italy-
that depressed nation suffering from
the fall of the last kingdom
-see that you have come
not to flirt with honour, but to marry it;
when the bravest knight shrinks back, you
charge in,
so that you will be celebrated: I say farewell.*

Second Lord

Health, at your bidding, serve your majesty!

*May health come to your Majesty when you call
it!*

KING

Those girls of Italy, take heed of them:
They say, our French lack language to deny,
If they demand: beware of being captives,
Before you serve.

*Look out for those Italian girls:
they say that the French cannot say no
to their offers: don't go getting taken prisoner
before you've even started fighting.*

Both

Our hearts receive your warnings.

We'll take your warning to heart.

KING

Farewell. Come hither to me.

Farewell. Come back to me.

Exit, attended

First Lord

O, my sweet lord, that you will stay behind us!

Oh, my sweet lord, why do you have to stay behind!

PAROLLES

'Tis not his fault, the spark.

It's not the lad's fault.

Second Lord

O, 'tis brave wars!

Oh, how exciting to be going to war!

PAROLLES

Most admirable: I have seen those wars.

Yes, wonderful: I've been to war.

BERTRAM

I am commanded here, and kept a coil with
'Too young' and 'the next year' and "tis too
early.'

*I am ordered to stay here, and tied up with
'you're too young' and 'maybe next year' and
'it's too early.'*

PAROLLES

An thy mind stand to't, boy, steal away bravely.

And you're thinking of sneaking away to the war.

BERTRAM

I shall stay here the forehorse to a smock,
Creaking my shoes on the plain masonry,
Till honour be bought up and no sword worn
But one to dance with! By heaven, I'll steal
away.

*If I stay here I'll be bossed around by women,
wearing my shoes out on the palace floors,
until there is no honour left and the only sword
I'll wear
will be a dress one! By God, I'll run away.*

First Lord

There's honour in the theft.

It would be an honourable crime.

PAROLLES

Commit it, count.

Do it, count.

Second Lord

I am your accessary; and so, farewell.

I am your accomplice; and so, goodbye.

BERTRAM

I grow to you, and our parting is a tortured body.

I lean out to you, and parting tears me apart.

First Lord

Farewell, captain.

Farewell, captain.

Second Lord
Sweet Monsieur Parolles!

Sweet Monsieur Parolles!

PAROLLES
Noble heroes, my sword and yours are kin.
Good
sparks and lustrous, a word, good metals: you
shall
find in the regiment of the Spinii one Captain
Spurio, with his cicatrice, an emblem of war,
here
on his sinister cheek; it was this very sword
entrenched it: say to him, I live; and observe his
reports for me.

*My noble heroes, you are my brothers in arms.
Good
lads and true, you're made of good stuff: you
will
find in the Spinii Regiment one captain Spurio,
who has a scar, a war wound, here
on his left cheek; it was this sword right here
which cut it: tell him I'm still alive; and tell me
how he reacts.*

First Lord
We shall, noble captain.

We shall, noble captain.

Exeunt Lords

PAROLLES
Mars dote on you for his novices! what will ye
do?

*The God of War wants you for an apprentice!
What will you do?*

BERTRAM
Stay: the king.

Hush: here's the King.

**Re-enter KING. BERTRAM and
PAROLLES retire**

PAROLLES
[To BERTRAM] Use a more spacious ceremony
to the
noble lords; you have restrained yourself within
the
list of too cold an adieu: be more expressive to
them: for they wear themselves in the cap of the
time, there do muster true gait, eat, speak, and
move under the influence of the most received
star;
and though the devil lead the measure, such are
to
be followed: after them, and take a more dilated
farewell.

*You should be more fulsome to the noble lords;
you have limited yourself to
too cold a goodbye: be warmer towards them:
for they are following the right path,
they are walking well, eating, speaking and
moving
under the influence of the best loved star;
even if the devil is leading the dance they should
be followed: go after them, and say a fuller
goodbye.*

BERTRAM
And I will do so.

I shall do so.

PAROLLES
Worthy fellows; and like to prove most sinewy
sword-men.

*They are good chaps, and likely to make
excellent soldiers.*

Exeunt BERTRAM and PAROLLES

Enter LAFEU

LAFEU
[Kneeling] Pardon, my lord, for me and for my
tidings.

Forgive me, my lord, for the news that I bring.

KING
I'll fee thee to stand up.

I'd like you to stand up.

LAFEU
Then here's a man stands, that has brought his
pardon.
I would you had kneel'd, my lord, to ask me
mercy,
And that at my bidding you could so stand up.

*Then here stands a man who has bought a
pardon.
I wish you had kneeled, my lord, to ask me for
mercy,
so that I could give you permission to stand.*

KING
I would I had; so I had broke thy pate,
And ask'd thee mercy for't.

*I wish I had, I wish I'd smacked you on the head
and asked you for mercy.*

LAFEU
Good faith, across: but, my good lord 'tis thus;
Will you be cured of your infirmity?

*By heaven, a good answer: but, my good lord,
this is how it stands;
do you want to be cured of your illness?*

KING
No.

No.

LAFEU
O, will you eat no grapes, my royal fox?
Yes, but you will my noble grapes, an if
My royal fox could reach them: I have seen a
medicine
That's able to breathe life into a stone,
Quicken a rock, and make you dance canary
With spritely fire and motion; whose simple
touch,
Is powerful to araise King Pepin, nay,

*Oh so my royal fox will have no grapes?
Yes, you will want the grapes I offer,
if the Royal Fox can get them: I have seen a
medicine
that can breathe life into a stone,
get a rock moving, can make you dance
a passionate lively jig; a drop of this
would resurrect King Pepin,
or get great Charlemagne to take up his pen*

To give great Charlemain a pen in's hand,
And write to her a love-line.

and write her a love letter.

KING
What 'her' is this?

Who is the 'her' you refer to?

LAFEU
Why, Doctor She: my lord, there's one arrived,
If you will see her: now, by my faith and honour,
If seriously I may convey my thoughts
In this my light deliverance, I have spoke
With one that, in her sex, her years, profession,
Wisdom and constancy, hath amazed me more
Than I dare blame my weakness: will you see her
For that is her demand, and know her business?
That done, laugh well at me.

*Why, she's a doctor: my lord, she has come here,
if you will see her: now, by my faith and honor,
if I can speak seriously
in this light-hearted tone, I have spoken
To one who for her sex, her age, her profession,
her wisdom and loyalty, has impressed me more
than could be accounted for by any bias: will you see her
and discover what she wants, for that is what she asks? There, I've said it, have a good laugh.*

KING
Now, good Lafeu,
Bring in the admiration; that we with thee
May spend our wonder too, or take off thine
By wondering how thou took'st it.

*Now then, good Lafeu,
bring in this miracle, so we can be amazed
like you, or stop your amazement
by questioning what you think is so special.*

LAFEU
Nay, I'll fit you,
And not be all day neither.

*You watch, I'll show you,
and I won't be all day about it either.*

Exit

KING
Thus he his special nothing ever prologues.

He always says this about his nonsenses.

Re-enter LAFEU, with HELENA

LAFEU
Nay, come your ways.

Now come along.

KING
This haste hath wings indeed.

Well, that was pretty quick.

LAFEU
Nay, come your ways:
This is his majesty; say your mind to him:

*Now, come along:
this is his Majesty; tell him what's on your mind:*

A traitor you do look like; but such traitors
His majesty seldom fears: I am Cressid's uncle,
That dare leave two together; fare you well.

*you look like a traitor; but his Majesty doesn't
fear traitors like you: I am like Cressida's uncle,
I don't worry about leaving you two together;
good luck.*

Exit

KING
Now, fair one, does your business follow us?

*Now, beautiful lady, has your business got
anything to do with us?*

HELENA
Ay, my good lord.
Gerard de Narbon was my father;
In what he did profess, well found.

*It has my good lord.
Gerard de Narbon was my father;
a well respected man in his profession.*

KING
I knew him.

I knew him.

HELENA
The rather will I spare my praises towards him:
Knowing him is enough. On's bed of death
Many receipts he gave me: chiefly one.
Which, as the dearest issue of his practise,
And of his old experience the oily darling,
He bade me store up, as a triple eye,
Safer than mine own two, more dear; I have so;
And hearing your high majesty is touch'd
With that malignant cause wherein the honour
Of my dear father's gift stands chief in power,
I come to tender it and my appliance
With all bound humbleness.

*Then I will not waste your time praising him:
if you knew him you know how good he was. On
his deathbed he gave me many recipes:
especially one, which was the greatest thing he
ever made, the triumph of his whole career,
and he told me to value it like a third eye,
to keep it safer than my own two, more valued; I
have done so, and hearing your Majesty is
suffering from that terrible illness which is the
one my dear father's gift is most effective
against I have come to offer it and my nursing
with all due respect.*

KING
We thank you, maiden;
But may not be so credulous of cure,
When our most learned doctors leave us and
The congregated college have concluded
That labouring art can never ransom nature
From her inaidible estate; I say we must not
So stain our judgment, or corrupt our hope,
To prostitute our past-cure malady
To empirics, or to dissever so
Our great self and our credit, to esteem
A senseless help when help past sense we deem.

*We thank you, girl;
but I don't have your faith in this cure,
when our most educated doctors have given up
and the whole University has decided
that their work cannot divert nature
from taking her course; I do not want
to be so foolish, or hold out false hopes,
by renting out this fatal illness
for quacks to experiment with, or to give up my
reputation and self-esteem by clutching at
straws when I know all hope is lost.*

HELENA
My duty then shall pay me for my pains:

Well at least I can say that I have tried:

I will no more enforce mine office on you.
Humbly entreating from your royal thoughts
A modest one, to bear me back again.

I won't force myself on you any more.
All I ask from your Highness is a small
Acknowledgement that I'm trying my best.

KING

I cannot give thee less, to be call'd grateful:
Thou thought'st to help me; and such thanks I give
As one near death to those that wish him live:
But what at full I know, thou know'st no part,
I knowing all my peril, thou no art.

It would be ungrateful to give you any less:
you meant well; and I give you the thanks
of a dying man to those who want him to live:
but you know nothing and I know everything,
I know the danger I'm in, and you don't know
medicine.

HELENA

What I can do can do no hurt to try,
Since you set up your rest 'gainst remedy.
He that of greatest works is finisher
Oft does them by the weakest minister:
So holy writ in babes hath judgment shown,
When judges have been babes; great floods have flown
From simple sources, and great seas have dried
When miracles have by the greatest been denied.
Oft expectation fails and most oft there
Where most it promises, and oft it hits
Where hope is coldest and despair most fits.

It can't do you any harm to try,
since you think nothing will do any good.
The one who has made the greatest works,
often performs them through the weakest
servant: so in the Bible babies have shown
wisdom when wise men have been like babies;
great floods have come
from little streams, and great seas have dried up
when the greatest have said that miracles can't
happen.
Hope often fails when you think it must come,
and it often comes when you least expect it.

KING

I must not hear thee; fare thee well, kind maid;
Thy pains not used must by thyself be paid:
Proffers not took reap thanks for their reward.

I mustn't listen to you; farewell, kind maid;
you must reward yourself for your unwanted
efforts;
unwanted offers still get thanks as their reward.

HELENA

Inspired merit so by breath is barr'd:
It is not so with Him that all things knows
As 'tis with us that square our guess by shows;
But most it is presumption in us when
The help of heaven we count the act of men.
Dear sir, to my endeavours give consent;
Of heaven, not me, make an experiment.
I am not an impostor that proclaim
Myself against the level of mine aim;
But know I think and think I know most sure
My art is not past power nor you past cure.

And so a man rejects inspired goodness:
it is not so with Him who knows all things
as it is with us, who demand to see evidence;
but it is arrogant of us
to see divine help as being the acts of men.
Dear sir, give your permission for me to try;
you will be testing heaven, not me.
I am not a fraud who is claiming
that I am as great as my target;
but I know that I think and I think I definitely
know that my efforts can win and that you can
be cured.

KING

Are thou so confident? within what space
Hopest thou my cure?

You are that confident? How long
do you think it would take you to cure me?

HELENA

The great'st grace lending grace
Ere twice the horses of the sun shall bring
Their fiery torcher his diurnal ring,
Ere twice in murk and occidental damp
Moist Hesperus hath quench'd his sleepy lamp,
Or four and twenty times the pilot's glass
Hath told the thievish minutes how they pass,
What is infirm from your sound parts shall fly,
Health shall live free and sickness freely die.

With the help of God
before the horses of the sun have pulled
their fiery burden twice round his circuit,
before the evening Star has twice
extinguished his nightlight in the murk and
Eastern damp,
or twenty-four times the sailor's timer
has counted off the passing minutes,
all weakness shall leave your healthy body;
health will flourish and sickness will die.

KING

Upon thy certainty and confidence
What darest thou venture?

What would you bet
on your certainty?

HELENA

Tax of impudence,
A strumpet's boldness, a divulged shame
Traduced by odious ballads: my maiden's name
Sear'd otherwise; nay, worse--if worse--
extended
With vilest torture let my life be ended.

A horrible penalty,
the brazenness of a whore, a revealed shame
Sung about in bawdy songs: my honour
as a virgin smeared; no and worse-if it is worse-
I will offer;
let my life be ended by the most horrible torture.

KING

Methinks in thee some blessed spirit doth speak
His powerful sound within an organ weak:
And what impossibility would slay
In common sense, sense saves another way.
Thy life is dear; for all that life can rate
Worth name of life in thee hath estimate,
Youth, beauty, wisdom, courage, all
That happiness and prime can happy call:
Thou this to hazard needs must intimate
Skill infinite or monstrous desperate.
Sweet practiser, thy physic I will try,
That ministers thine own death if I die.

I think perhaps some blessed spirit is speaking
through you, a powerful sound from a small
instrument: and what common sense would say
is impossible another sort of sense says is
possible. Your life is valuable; for everything
that represents life is present in you,
youth, beauty, wisdom, courage, all
the things that bring us happiness;
that you are prepared to risk this shows
either that you have wonderful skill or are
desperate.
Sweet practitioner, I will try your medicine,
and if I die it will bring death to you.

HELENA

If I break time, or flinch in property
Of what I spoke, unpitied let me die,
And well deserved: not helping, death's my fee;
But, if I help, what do you promise me?

If I break my word, or cannot prove
what I promised, let me die an unpitied
and well-deserved death: if I don't help, pay me
with death;
but, if it works, what will you give me?

KING
Make thy demand.

Ask what you want.

HELENA
But will you make it even?

But will you keep the bargain?

KING
Ay, by my sceptre and my hopes of heaven.

Yes, I swear by my sceptre and my hopes of getting to heaven.

HELENA
Then shalt thou give me with thy kingly hand
What husband in thy power I will command:
Exempted be from me the arrogance
To choose from forth the royal blood of France,
My low and humble name to propagate
With any branch or image of thy state;
But such a one, thy vassal, whom I know
Is free for me to ask, thee to bestow.

*Then you shall give me with your royal hand
any husband I ask for whom you have the power
to give: I promise I won't have the arrogance
to choose from the French royal family,
to try and mix my low and humble name
with any part of your family;
but any other amongst your subjects, whom I know
it is acceptable for me to ask for, you must give.*

KING
Here is my hand; the premises observed,
Thy will by my performance shall be served:
So make the choice of thy own time, for I,
Thy resolved patient, on thee still rely.
More should I question thee, and more I must,
Though more to know could not be more to trust,
From whence thou camest, how tended on: but rest
Unquestion'd welcome and undoubted blest.
Give me some help here, ho! If thou proceed
As high as word, my deed shall match thy meed.

*Here's my hand on it; the terms are set,
you will be rewarded proportional to my
recovery: so choose your time, for I
commit myself to you as your patient, and rely
on you. I would like to ask you some more
questions, although nothing you could say could
increase my trust in you,
I want to know where you come from, who looks
after you: but rest
assured of your welcome and my blessing.
Hey! Give me some help here! If you do
as well as you promise I will pay your just
reward.*

Flourish. Exeunt

SCENE II. Rousillon. The COUNT's palace.

Enter COUNTESS and Clown

COUNTESS
Come on, sir; I shall now put you to the height of
your breeding.

Come on, sir; I'm going to put you through your paces.

Clown
I will show myself highly fed and lowly taught: I
know my business is but to the court.

*I'll show you that I'm well fed and badly taught: I
know that I should be at court.*

COUNTESS
To the court! why, what place make you special,
when you put off that with such contempt? But
to the court!

*The court! What's made you so special
when you can just lightly say that? The court!*

Clown
Truly, madam, if God have lent a man any
manners, he
may easily put it off at court: he that cannot
make
a leg, put off's cap, kiss his hand and say
nothing,
has neither leg, hands, lip, nor cap; and indeed
such a fellow, to say precisely, were not for the
court; but for me, I have an answer will serve all
men.

*Honestly, madam, if God has given a man any
manners, he
can fit right in at court: the one who can't
bend the knee, doff his cap, kiss his hand and
say nothing
doesn't have knees, hands, lips or a cap; and in
fact to be precise about it a chap like that
wouldn't fit
at court; but as for me, I have an answer for
everything.*

COUNTESS
Marry, that's a bountiful answer that fits all
questions.

*I say, that's a good answer that would fit all
questions.*

Clown
It is like a barber's chair that fits all buttocks,
the pin-buttock, the quatch-buttock, the brawn
buttock, or any buttock.

*It's like a barber's chair that fits all backsides,
skinny ones, squashy ones, muscular ones
or any others.*

COUNTESS
Will your answer serve fit to all questions?

And your answer will fit all questions?

Clown
As fit as ten groats is for the hand of an attorney,

It fits like money in the hand of a lawyer,

as your French crown for your taffeta punk, as Tib's
rush for Tom's forefinger, as a pancake for Shrove
Tuesday, a morris for May-day, as the nail to his
hole, the cuckold to his horn, as a scolding queen
to a wrangling knave, as the nun's lip to the
friar's mouth, nay, as the pudding to his skin.

as the clap for a showy fop, like a ring of rushes on a peasant's finger, like a pancake on Shrove Tuesday, a morris dance on May Day, like a nail in itshole, a cuckold with his horn, a scolding Queen to an arguing scoundrel, the nun's lip to the friar's mouth, like the pudding to its skin.

COUNTESS
Have you, I say, an answer of such fitness for all questions?

I'm asking you do you have an answer to fit all questions?

Clown
From below your duke to beneath your constable, it
will fit any question.

From below a Duke to below your steward, it will fit any question.

COUNTESS
It must be an answer of most monstrous size that must fit all demands.

It must be an incredibly large answer if it suits everything.

Clown
But a trifle neither, in good faith, if the learned should speak truth of it: here it is, and all that belongs to't. Ask me if I am a courtier: it shall do you no harm to learn.

It's just trifle, honestly, if the educated tell the truth of it: here it is, with everything about it. Ask me if I am a courtier: it will do you no harm to learn.

COUNTESS
To be young again, if we could: I will be a fool in
question, hoping to be the wiser by your answer. I
pray you, sir, are you a courtier?

I'd like to learn to be young again if it was possible: I will be a fool in my question, hoping that you will give me a wiser answer. Tell me Sir, are you a courtier?

Clown
O Lord, sir! There's a simple putting off. More, more, a hundred of them.

Oh Lord, sir! There's a simple way of doing it. Ask me more, a hundred of them.

COUNTESS
Sir, I am a poor friend of yours, that loves you.

Sir, I am a poor friend of yours, who loves you.

Clown
O Lord, sir! Thick, thick, spare not me.

Oh Lord, sir! Come on, more, don't spare me.

COUNTESS

I think, sir, you can eat none of this homely meat.

I think, sir, that you will not eat this simple meat.

Clown

O Lord, sir! Nay, put me to't, I warrant you.

Oh Lord, sir! No, come on, really test me.

COUNTESS

You were lately whipped, sir, as I think.

You were recently whipped, sir, I believe.

Clown

O Lord, sir! spare not me.

Oh Lord, sir! Do not spare me.

COUNTESS

Do you cry, 'O Lord, sir!' at your whipping, and 'spare not me?' Indeed your 'O Lord, sir!' is very sequent to your whipping: you would answer very well
to a whipping, if you were but bound to't.

Do you cry, 'oh Lord, sir!' when you are whipped, and 'don't spare me?' In fact your 'oh Lord, sir!' follows on very closely to your whipping: you would have a very good answer for a whipping, if you were handed one.

Clown

I ne'er had worse luck in my life in my 'O Lord, sir!' I see things may serve long, but not serve ever.

I never had such bad luck with my 'oh Lord, sir!' I see things will work for a long time but not for ever.

COUNTESS

I play the noble housewife with the time
To entertain't so merrily with a fool.

*Here I am messing around as if
I have the time to amuse myself with a fool.*

Clown

O Lord, sir! why, there't serves well again.

'Oh Lord, sir!' Why look, now it's working well again.

COUNTESS

An end, sir; to your business. Give Helen this,
And urge her to a present answer back:
Commend me to my kinsmen and my son:
This is not much.

That's enough of that; get on with your business. Give this to Helen, and tell her that I want an answer: give my regards to my kinsmen and my son: it's not much to ask.

Clown

Not much commendation to them.

You don't want me to give them much regards then.

COUNTESS

Not much employment for you: you understand me?

Not much for you to do: do you understand?

Clown

Most fruitfully: I am there before my legs.

COUNTESS
Haste you again.

Exeunt severally

Absolutely: I'll be there before you know it.

Hurry back.

SCENE III. Paris. The KING's palace.

Enter BERTRAM, LAFEU, and PAROLLES

LAFEU
They say miracles are past; and we have our
philosophical persons, to make modern and
familiar,
things supernatural and causeless. Hence is it
that
we make trifles of terrors, ensconcing ourselves
into seeming knowledge, when we should
submit
ourselves to an unknown fear.

They say there are no more miracles; and we have our scientists to make supernatural and unexplainable things seem modern and familiar. And so we disregard terrors, burying ourselves in what we think we know, when actually we should be feeling some unknown fear.

PAROLLES
Why, 'tis the rarest argument of wonder that
hath
shot out in our latter times.

Why, it's the greatest miracle that has happened in our times.

BERTRAM
And so 'tis.

That's true.

LAFEU
To be relinquish'd of the artists,--

To be given up on by the skilled ones-

PAROLLES
So I say.

That's what I mean.

LAFEU
Both of Galen and Paracelsus.

By both Galen and Paracelus.

PAROLLES
So I say.

That's what I'm talking about.

LAFEU
Of all the learned and authentic fellows,--

Of all the genuine learned men-

PAROLLES
Right; so I say.

Yes, that's what I've been saying.

LAFEU
That gave him out incurable,--

They said that he was incurable-

PAROLLES

Why, there 'tis; so say I too.

Yes, I know; that's what I've said.

LAFEU
Not to be helped,--

That he couldn't be helped-

PAROLLES
Right; as 'twere, a man assured of a—

Right; he was a man who had been promised-

LAFEU
Uncertain life, and sure death.

An uncertain life, and certain death.

PAROLLES
Just, you say well; so would I have said.

That's it, you've hit the nail on the head; that's just what I would have said.

LAFEU
I may truly say, it is a novelty to the world.

I really must say, it's quite unheard-of.

PAROLLES
It is, indeed: if you will have it in showing, you shall read it in--what do you call there?

It is, indeed: if you want the proof of it you shall read it in-what to call it?

LAFEU
A showing of a heavenly effect in an earthly actor.

Divine work on a mortal being.

PAROLLES
That's it; I would have said the very same.

That's the one; just what I would have said.

LAFEU
Why, your dolphin is not lustier: 'fore me, I speak in respect—

Why, a dolphin has less energy: I must say, I'm talking about-

PAROLLES
Nay, 'tis strange, 'tis very strange, that is the brief and the tedious of it; and he's of a most facinerious spirit that will not acknowledge it to be the—

No, it's strange, it's very strange, that's the long and the short of it: and it would take someone with a very wicked spirit to deny that it is-

LAFEU
Very hand of heaven.

Truly the hand of God.

PAROLLES
Ay, so I say.

Yes, that's what I say.

LAFEU

In a most weak—

pausing

and debile minister, great power, great transcendence: which should, indeed, give us a further use to be made than alone the recovery of
the king, as to be--

pausing

generally thankful.

PAROLLES
I would have said it; you say well. Here comes the king.

In a very weak–	
(pause)	
And feeble worker, there is great power, unimaginable knowledge: and in fact we should use it for other things apart from just saving the King, so we can be–	
(pause)	
generally grateful.	
That's what I would have said; you've said it well. Here comes the King.	

Enter KING, HELENA, and Attendants. LAFEU and PAROLLES retire

LAFEU
Lustig, as the Dutchman says: I'll like a maid the better, whilst I have a tooth in my head: why, he's
able to lead her a coranto.

Lustig (full of health), as a Dutchman would say: I'll like a girl better, whilst I still have teeth: why, he's able to run ahead of her.

PAROLLES
Mort du vinaigre! is not this Helen?

Good gracious! Isn't that Helen?

LAFEU
'Fore God, I think so.

By God, I think it is

KING
Go, call before me all the lords in court.
Sit, my preserver, by thy patient's side;
And with this healthful hand, whose banish'd sense
Thou hast repeal'd, a second time receive
The confirmation of my promised gift,
Which but attends thy naming.

Go and summon to me all the Lords of the court. Sit down, you lifesaver, at your patient's side; and from this healthy hand, whose numbness you have removed, take for a second time the assurance that I will give what I promised, I'm just waiting for you to say what you want.

Enter three or four Lords

Fair maid, send forth thine eye: this youthful parcel
Of noble bachelors stand at my bestowing,

Fair maid, look them over: all these young noble bachelors are mine to give, I have the power of a king and of a father

O'er whom both sovereign power and father's voice
I have to use: thy frank election make;
Thou hast power to choose, and they none to forsake.

HELENA
To each of you one fair and virtuous mistress
Fall, when Love please! marry, to each, but one!

LAFEU
I'ld give bay Curtal and his furniture,
My mouth no more were broken than these boys',
And writ as little beard.

KING
Peruse them well:
Not one of those but had a noble father.

HELENA
Gentlemen, Heaven hath through me restored the king to health.

All
We understand it, and thank heaven for you.

HELENA
I am a simple maid, and therein wealthiest,
That I protest I simply am a maid.
Please it your majesty, I have done already:
The blushes in my cheeks thus whisper me,
'We blush that thou shouldst choose; but, be refused,
Let the white death sit on thy cheek for ever;
We'll ne'er come there again.'

KING
Make choice; and, see,
Who shuns thy love shuns all his love in me.

HELENA
Now, Dian, from thy altar do I fly,
And to imperial Love, that god most high,
Do my sighs stream.

over them: choose whichever you want, you have the power of selection, and none of them can say no.

May each of you get a fair and virtuous mistress when love thinks the time is right! Just one for each, mind you!

I'd give my bay horse and his saddlery, to have a full set of teeth like these boys, and to be as freshfaced.

Look them over carefully, every one of them has a noble father.

Gentlemen, through me heaven has given the King back his health.

We know that, and we thank heaven for you.

*I am a simple maid, and that's my proudest boast,
that I am simply a maid.
If your Majesty permits, I have already chosen:
the blushes in my cheeks whisper to me,
'we are blushing at your choice; but if you are refused, then white death will sit on your cheek forever; we will never be back.'*

Make your choice, and I promise that anyone who rejects your love is rejecting mine as well.

Now, Diana, I fly away from your altar, and go to the emperor of love, the highest god, that's where my prayers are going now.

Sir, will you hear my suit?

Sir, will you listen to my request?

First Lord
And grant it.

And give it.

HELENA
Thanks, sir; all the rest is mute.

Thank you sir; the rest is silence.

LAFEU
I had rather be in this choice than throw ames-
ace
for my life.

*I would rather be part of this selection than
throw a double one
for my life.*

HELENA
The honour, sir, that flames in your fair eyes,
Before I speak, too threateningly replies:
Love make your fortunes twenty times above
Her that so wishes and her humble love!

*The honour, sir, that is burning in your fair
eyes, answers me too threateningly before I
speak: may love give you something twenty
times better than the one who wishes that for
you and her humble love.*

Second Lord
No better, if you please.

*I don't want any better than you, if that's
allowed.*

HELENA
My wish receive,
Which great Love grant! and so, I take my
leave.

*Take my best wishes for that,
and I hope the god of love grants it! And so, I'm
going.*

LAFEU
Do all they deny her? An they were sons of
mine,
I'd have them whipped; or I would send them to
the
Turk, to make eunuchs of.

*Are they all refusing her? If they were sons of
mine
I'd have them whipped; or I would send them to
the
Turks, to have them made into eunuchs.*

HELENA
Be not afraid that I your hand should take;
I'll never do you wrong for your own sake:
Blessing upon your vows! and in your bed
Find fairer fortune, if you ever wed!

*Don't be afraid that I would take your hand;
I would never want to do harm:
may your marriage be blessed! And may you
find someone more beautiful in your bed, if you
ever marry!*

LAFEU
These boys are boys of ice, they'll none have
her:
sure, they are bastards to the English; the French
ne'er got 'em.

*These boys are made of ice, none of them will
have her:
I'm certain they are the bastard sons of
Englishmen; no Frenchman
ever fathered these.*

HELENA

You are too young, too happy, and too good,
To make yourself a son out of my blood.

You are too young, too happy, and too good,
to breed a son from me.

Fourth Lord

Fair one, I think not so.

Beautiful one, I don't agree.

LAFEU

There's one grape yet; I am sure thy father drunk
wine: but if thou be'st not an ass, I am a youth
of fourteen; I have known thee already.

There's just one left; I am sure your father put
good blood in you but if you're not an ass then I
am a fourteen-year-old; I know what you're like.

HELENA

[To BERTRAM] I dare not say I take you; but I
give
Me and my service, ever whilst I live,
Into your guiding power. This is the man.

I dare not say that I am taking you; but I give
myself and my service, as long as I live,
into your hands. This is the man.

KING

Why, then, young Bertram, take her; she's thy
wife.

Why then, young Bertram, take her; she's your
wife.

BERTRAM

My wife, my liege! I shall beseech your
highness,
In such a business give me leave to use
The help of mine own eyes.

My wife, my lord! I must ask your Highness
that in a business like this you let me
make my own choices.

KING

Know'st thou not, Bertram,
What she has done for me?

Bertram, don't you know
what she has done for me?

BERTRAM

Yes, my good lord;
But never hope to know why I should marry her.

I do know that my good lord;
but I can't see why I should marry her.

KING

Thou know'st she has raised me from my sickly
bed.

You know that she has raised me from my sick
bed.

BERTRAM

But follows it, my lord, to bring me down
Must answer for your raising? I know her well:
She had her breeding at my father's charge.
A poor physician's daughter my wife! Disdain

But must it follow, my lord, that I have to be
brought down to pay for you being raised up? I
know her well: she was brought up at my
father's expense. Me, marry the daughter of a

Rather corrupt me ever!

KING

'Tis only title thou disdain'st in her, the which
I can build up. Strange is it that our bloods,
Of colour, weight, and heat, pour'd all together,
Would quite confound distinction, yet stand off
In differences so mighty. If she be
All that is virtuous, save what thou dislikest,
A poor physician's daughter, thou dislikest
Of virtue for the name: but do not so:
From lowest place when virtuous things proceed,
The place is dignified by the doer's deed:
Where great additions swell's, and virtue none,
It is a dropsied honour. Good alone
Is good without a name. Vileness is so:
The property by what it is should go,
Not by the title. She is young, wise, fair;

In these to nature she's immediate heir,
And these breed honour: that is honour's scorn,
Which challenges itself as honour's born
And is not like the sire: honours thrive,
When rather from our acts we them derive
Than our foregoers: the mere word's a slave
Debosh'd on every tomb, on every grave
A lying trophy, and as oft is dumb
Where dust and damn'd oblivion is the tomb
Of honour'd bones indeed. What should be said?
If thou canst like this creature as a maid,
I can create the rest: virtue and she
Is her own dower; honour and wealth from me.

BERTRAM

I cannot love her, nor will strive to do't.

KING

Thou wrong'st thyself, if thou shouldst strive to choose.

HELENA

That you are well restored, my lord, I'm glad:
Let the rest go.

KING

poor physician! I'd rather face your disapproval than be brought this low!

It's only her lack of title you don't like, and I can fix that. It is strange that our blood, if all poured together could not be distinguished by colour, weight or heat, and yet we claim that they are so different. If she is good in everything, except that which you dislike, the fact that she is a poor physician's daughter, then you dislike goodness just because of its name: do not do so: when good things come from humble places, the place is made better by what has been done. Where there are great titles, but no goodness, it is a diseased honour. Goodness is goodness, it doesn't need a title. Vileness is the same: you should judge things by their properties, not their names. She is young, wise, beautiful;

She inherits these things from nature, and they make honor: that is what honor scorns, which mocks itself when honor is inherited and the son is not like the father: honors are worth something when we get them from our actions rather than inheriting them: words are just slaves debased on every tomb, a lying trophy on every grave, and they are just as often silent when dust and terrible oblivion is the tomb of those who are really honourable. What can I say? If you like this creature as a woman, I can do the rest: in terms of goodness she brings her own dowry; she will get honors and wealth from me.

I cannot love her, and I will not force myself to.

If you won't do this you're making a lot of trouble for yourself.

I'm glad that you are now in good health, my lord: forget about the rest.

My honour's at the stake; which to defeat,
I must produce my power. Here, take her hand,
Proud scornful boy, unworthy this good gift;
That dost in vile misprision shackle up
My love and her desert; that canst not dream,
We, poising us in her defective scale,
Shall weigh thee to the beam; that wilt not know,
It is in us to plant thine honour where
We please to have it grow. Cheque thy contempt:
Obey our will, which travails in thy good:
Believe not thy disdain, but presently
Do thine own fortunes that obedient right
Which both thy duty owes and our power claims;
Or I will throw thee from my care for ever
Into the staggers and the careless lapse
Of youth and ignorance; both my revenge and hate
Loosing upon thee, in the name of justice,
Without all terms of pity. Speak; thine answer.

BERTRAM
Pardon, my gracious lord; for I submit
My fancy to your eyes: when I consider
What great creation and what dole of honour
Flies where you bid it, I find that she, which late
Was in my nobler thoughts most base, is now
The praised of the king; who, so ennobled,
Is as 'twere born so.

KING
Take her by the hand,
And tell her she is thine: to whom I promise
A counterpoise, if not to thy estate
A balance more replete.

BERTRAM
I take her hand.

KING
Good fortune and the favour of the king
Smile upon this contract; whose ceremony
Shall seem expedient on the now-born brief,

My honour's at stake; to win here
I must use my power. Here, take her hand,
you arrogant contemptuous boy, who doesn't
deserve this good gift;
you are showing a revolting contempt for both
my love and what she deserves; you can't imagine
that you can show such contempt for us
and not face the consequences; don't you know
That it's up to me to assign honour
to whomever I please; rein in your contempt:
do as I order, which is for your own good:
do not follow your contempt, but now
do the right thing for your own fortune
which you're bound to by duty and my power
orders;
otherwise I will expel you from my care forever
into the stumbling careless errors
of youth and ignorance; I will unleash
both my revenge and my hate upon you
in the name of justice, I will show you no mercy.
Speak; give me your answer.

I apologise, my gracious lord; I now see it
from your point of view: when I think
that titles and honours are given by you, I
realise that she, who recently seemed to me in
my noble thoughts very humble, is now
praised by the King; as she is given this honour
it is as if she was always noble.

Take her by the hand
and tell her she is yours: I promise her
riches which, if they don't completely match
your estate
will make the two of you much more even.

I take her by the hand.

May good fortune and the King's favor
smile upon this agreement; now seems
a good time to perform the ceremony,

And be perform'd to-night: the solemn feast
Shall more attend upon the coming space,
Expecting absent friends. As thou lovest her,
Thy love's to me religious; else, does err.

Exeunt all but LAFEU and PAROLLES

LAFEU
[Advancing] Do you hear, monsieur? a word
with you.

PAROLLES
Your pleasure, sir?

LAFEU
Your lord and master did well to make his
recantation.

PAROLLES
Recantation! My lord! my master!

LAFEU
Ay; is it not a language I speak?

PAROLLES
A most harsh one, and not to be understood
without
bloody succeeding. My master!

LAFEU
Are you companion to the Count Rousillon?

PAROLLES
To any count, to all counts, to what is man.

LAFEU
To what is count's man: count's master is of
another style.

PAROLLES
You are too old, sir; let it satisfy you, you are
too old.

LAFEU
I must tell thee, sirrah, I write man; to which
title age cannot bring thee.

---

and they shall be married tonight: the solemn
feast shallbe postponed a little while,
to wait for absent friends. As you love her,
your love to me is sacred; anything else is
blasphemous.

Did you hear that, sir? A word with you.

What is it, sir?

Your lord and master did well to take that back.

Take it back! My Lord! My master!

Yes; am I not speaking a language you
understand?

A very harsh one, which can't be understood
without
bloodshed following. My master!

Aren't you a friend of the Count Rousillon?

I'm a friend to any counts, to all counts, to any
man.

A count's man is one thing: a count's master is
quite another.

You are too old to fight, sir; you should be glad
of that, you are too old.

I must tell you, sir, that I am a man; you won't
get that title through age.

PAROLLES

What I dare too well do, I dare not do.

I dare not do what I would really like to.

LAFEU

I did think thee, for two ordinaries, to be a pretty wise fellow; thou didst make tolerable vent of thy
travel; it might pass: yet the scarfs and the bannerets about thee did manifoldly dissuade me from
believing thee a vessel of too great a burthen. I have now found thee; when I lose thee again, I care
not: yet art thou good for nothing but taking up; and
that thou't scarce worth.

*I did think, for a little while, that you were a pretty
wise chap; you told a good story of your
travels; it was passable: but the scarves and
decorations on you certainly made me think
that you were pretty shallow. And I've
found out I was right; if I don't see you again
I wouldn't care: you're good for nothing but idle
chatter
and hardly much good at that.*

PAROLLES

Hadst thou not the privilege of antiquity upon thee,--

If you didn't have the privilege of age–

LAFEU

Do not plunge thyself too far in anger, lest thou hasten thy trial; which if--Lord have mercy on thee
for a hen! So, my good window of lattice, fare thee
well: thy casement I need not open, for I look through thee. Give me thy hand.

*Don't let your anger run on to far, in case
you have to back it up with action, if you do–
may the Lord
pity you for your suffering! So, you lattice
window,
farewell: I don't need to open your frame, I can
see through you. Give me your hand.*

PAROLLES

My lord, you give me most egregious indignity.

My lord, you have given me a serious insult.

LAFEU

Ay, with all my heart; and thou art worthy of it.

Yes, with all my heart; and you deserve it.

PAROLLES

I have not, my lord, deserved it.

I have not deserved it, my lord.

LAFEU

Yes, good faith, every dram of it; and I will not bate thee a scruple.

*You have indeed, every ounce of it; and I will
not lessen it by one drop.*

PAROLLES

Well, I shall be wiser.

Well, I shall be wiser.

LAFEU

Even as soon as thou canst, for thou hast to pull at
a smack o' the contrary. If ever thou be'st bound
in thy scarf and beaten, thou shalt find what it is
to be proud of thy bondage. I have a desire to hold
my acquaintance with thee, or rather my knowledge,
that I may say in the default, he is a man I know.

*You should become so as soon as you can, for you
are the opposite at the moment. If you're ever
tied up in your scarf and beaten, you will find
out what it means to be proud of your slavery. I
would like to keep
my acquaintance with you, or rather my
knowledge of you,
so that I can say when the time comes, I know
that man.*

PAROLLES

My lord, you do me most insupportable vexation.

My lord, you are being a great pain.

LAFEU

I would it were hell-pains for thy sake, and my poor
doing eternal: for doing I am past: as I will by
thee, in what motion age will give me leave.

*I wish for your sake they were the pains of hell,
and that my poor efforts would last forever: I
am beyond action, and I will be beyond you,
with whatever speed my age has left me.*

Exit

PAROLLES

Well, thou hast a son shall take this disgrace off
me; scurvy, old, filthy, scurvy lord! Well, I must
be patient; there is no fettering of authority.
I'll beat him, by my life, if I can meet him with
any convenience, an he were double and double a
lord. I'll have no more pity of his age than I
would of--I'll beat him, an if I could but meet
him again.

*Well, if you have a son I'll challenge him
instead;
vile, old, filthy, vile lord! Well, I must
be patient; I will have my rights.
I'll beat him, I swear, if I can get him
in a convenient place, if he were a lord four
times over.
I'll have no more pity for his age than I would
for—I'll beat him, if I could just see him again.*

Re-enter LAFEU

LAFEU

Sirrah, your lord and master's married; there's news
for you: you have a new mistress.

*Sir, your lord and master is married; there's
some news
for you: you have a new mistress.*

PAROLLES

I most unfeignedly beseech your lordship to make
some reservation of your wrongs: he is my good
lord: whom I serve above is my master.

*I must openly ask your lordship to correct
what you have just said: he is my good
lord: the one above, whom I serve, is my master.*

LAFEU
Who? God?

Who? God?

PAROLLES
Ay, sir.

Yes, sir.

LAFEU
The devil it is that's thy master. Why dost thou
garter up thy arms o' this fashion? dost make
hose of
sleeves? do other servants so? Thou wert best
set
thy lower part where thy nose stands. By mine
honour, if I were but two hours younger, I'ld
beat
thee: methinks, thou art a general offence, and
every man should beat thee: I think thou wast
created for men to breathe themselves upon
thee.

*It's the devil who is your master. Why do you
gather up your sleeves in this way? Do you
have stockings for sleeves? Do other servants?
You would be best
knocked head over heels. On my word, if I were
just two hours younger,
I would beat you: I think you are a public
nuisance, and
every man should beat you: I think you were
created for men to use you as a punchbag.*

PAROLLES
This is hard and undeserved measure, my lord.

*These are harsh words, my lord, and
undeserved.*

LAFEU
Go to, sir; you were beaten in Italy for picking a
kernel out of a pomegranate; you are a vagabond
and
no true traveller: you are more saucy with lords
and honourable personages than the commission
of your
birth and virtue gives you heraldry. You are not
worth another word, else I'ld call you knave. I
leave you.

*Get lost, sir; you were beaten in Italy for
stealing
pomegranate seeds; you are a tramp, not
a true traveller: you are more cheeky with lords
and noble men than the position of your birth
gives you any right to be. You are not
worth another word, if you were I'd call you a
knave. I leave you.*

Exit

PAROLLES
Good, very good; it is so then: good, very good;
let it be concealed awhile.

*Good, very good; that's the way it is: good, very
good;
we'll let it lie a while.*

Re-enter BERTRAM

BERTRAM
Undone, and forfeited to cares for ever!

Ruined, condemned to misery forever!

PAROLLES
What's the matter, sweet-heart?

What's the matter, dear boy?

BERTRAM
Although before the solemn priest I have sworn,
I will not bed her.

Although I have made my promise before the solemn priest, I won't sleep with her.

PAROLLES
What, what, sweet-heart?

What's all this, dear boy?

BERTRAM
O my Parolles, they have married me!
I'll to the Tuscan wars, and never bed her.

Oh my dear Parolles, they have married me! I'll go to the war in Tuscany, and never sleep with her.

PAROLLES
France is a dog-hole, and it no more merits
The tread of a man's foot: to the wars!

France is a pit, and it's not worth staying in: let's go to the war!

BERTRAM
There's letters from my mother: what the import is,
I know not yet.

*Here are letters from my mother: what she has to say
I don't yet know.*

PAROLLES
Ay, that would be known. To the wars, my boy, to the wars!
He wears his honour in a box unseen,
That hugs his kicky-wicky here at home,
Spending his manly marrow in her arms,
Which should sustain the bound and high curvet
Of Mars's fiery steed. To other regions
France is a stable; we that dwell in't jades;
Therefore, to the war!

*Yes, we'll find out. To the war, my boy, to the war!
A man cannot show his honor
who sits at home cuddling his mistress,
wasting his manly essence in her arms,
which he should be using to urge on
the fiery horse of Mars. Compared to other
regions France is a stable; we who stay here are
useless nags; so, let's go to the war!*

BERTRAM
It shall be so: I'll send her to my house,
Acquaint my mother with my hate to her,
And wherefore I am fled; write to the king
That which I durst not speak; his present gift
Shall furnish me to those Italian fields,
Where noble fellows strike: war is no strife
To the dark house and the detested wife.

*That's what we'll do: I'll send her to my house,
let my mother know how much I hate her,
and where I have run to; I will write to the King
the things I do not say to him; this gift of his
we'll send me to those Italian fields
where noble fellows battle: war is nothing
compared to a joyless house and a hated wife.*

PAROLLES
Will this capriccio hold in thee? art sure?

Will you stick to this? Are you certain?

BERTRAM

Go with me to my chamber, and advise me.
I'll send her straight away: to-morrow
I'll to the wars, she to her single sorrow.

PAROLLES

Why, these balls bound; there's noise in it. 'Tis
hard:
A young man married is a man that's marr'd:
Therefore away, and leave her bravely; go:
The king has done you wrong: but, hush, 'tis so.

Exeunt

Come to my room with me and advise me.
I'll send her away at once: tomorrow
I'll go to the war, and she can go to her
spinsterhood.

Why, these balls bounce; there is substance in it.
It's a hard thing:
a young man who is married is a man who is
spoilt:
so get going, have the courage to leave her; go:
the King has done you wrong: that's a fact.

SCENE IV. Paris. The KING's palace.

Enter HELENA and Clown

HELENA
My mother greets me kindly; is she well?

My mother sends me kind greetings; is she well?

Clown
She is not well; but yet she has her health: she's very merry; but yet she is not well: but thanks be given, she's very well and wants nothing i', the world; but yet she is not well.

She is not well; but she's healthy: she's very happy; but she's not well: but thank goodness she's very well and wants for nothing; however she is not well.

HELENA
If she be very well, what does she ail, that she's not very well?

If she's very well, what's wrong with her, that makes her not well?

Clown
Truly, she's very well indeed, but for two things.

She is really very well indeed, except for two things.

HELENA
What two things?

What two things?

Clown
One, that she's not in heaven, whither God send her
quickly! the other that she's in earth, from whence
God send her quickly!

*One, that she's not in heaven, may God send her there
quickly! The other is that she is on earth, may God
send her from here quickly!*

Enter PAROLLES

PAROLLES
Bless you, my fortunate lady!

Bless you, lucky lady!

HELENA
I hope, sir, I have your good will to have mine own
good fortunes.

I hope, Sir, that you are happy for me to be lucky.

PAROLLES
You had my prayers to lead them on; and to keep them
on, have them still. O, my knave, how does my old lady?

I prayed for you to be lucky, and now I pray for you to stay lucky. Oh, knave, how is my former lady?

Clown

So that you had her wrinkles and I her money,
I would she did as you say.

If you could have her wrinkles and I could have
her money, I'd like her to be as you said.

PAROLLES

Why, I say nothing.

But I said nothing.

Clown

Marry, you are the wiser man; for many a man's
tongue shakes out his master's undoing: to say
nothing, to do nothing, to know nothing, and to
have
nothing, is to be a great part of your title; which
is within a very little of nothing.

That makes you a wise man; many men's
tongues are the downfall of their masters: to say
nothing, to do nothing, to know nothing, and to
have
nothing, is a very important part of your
position; which basically amounts to nothing.

PAROLLES

Away! thou'rt a knave.

Get lost! You're a knave.

Clown

You should have said, sir, before a knave thou'rt
a
knave; that's, before me thou'rt a knave: this had
been truth, sir.

You should have said, sir, that before a knave
you are
a knave; meaning, you were a knave before I
was: that would be the truth, sir.

PAROLLES

Go to, thou art a witty fool; I have found thee.

Get away, you are a witty fool; I know your sort.

Clown

Did you find me in yourself, sir? or were you
taught to find me? The search, sir, was
profitable;
and much fool may you find in you, even to the
world's pleasure and the increase of laughter.

Do you see me in yourself, sir? Or were you
taught to be like me? It was a successful lesson,
sir;
and may you find much of the fool in you, for the
world's pleasure and more laughter.

PAROLLES

A good knave, i' faith, and well fed.
Madam, my lord will go away to-night;
A very serious business calls on him.
The great prerogative and rite of love,
Which, as your due, time claims, he does
acknowledge;
But puts it off to a compell'd restraint;
Whose want, and whose delay, is strew'd with
sweets,
Which they distil now in the curbed time,

I must say this is a good knave, well fed too.
Madam, my lord must go away tonight;
he has some very serious business to attend to.
He knows that you have a right to the
full rights of
marriage;
but he has been forced to put it off;
but the delay will make it all the
sweeter,
the pleasures will be refined in the extra time,

To make the coming hour o'erflow with joy
And pleasure drown the brim.

HELENA
What's his will else?

PAROLLES
That you will take your instant leave o' the king
And make this haste as your own good proceeding,
Strengthen'd with what apology you think
May make it probable need.

HELENA
What more commands he?

PAROLLES
That, having this obtain'd, you presently
Attend his further pleasure.

HELENA
In every thing I wait upon his will.

PAROLLES
I shall report it so.

HELENA
I pray you.

Exit PAROLLES

Come, sirrah.

Exeunt

so that when the hour comes your cup will overflow with joy.

What else does he want?

That you will leave the King at once and get away as quickly as possible, giving whatever apology you think is appropriate.

What else does he order?

That once you have permission to go you wait for his further orders.

I wait for his commands in everything.

I will tell him this.

Please do.

Come on sir.

SCENE V. Paris. The KING's palace.

Enter LAFEU and BERTRAM

LAFEU
But I hope your lordship thinks not him a soldier.

But I hope your lordship does not think he is a soldier.

BERTRAM
Yes, my lord, and of very valiant approof.

He is, my lord, and one who has proved very brave.

LAFEU
You have it from his own deliverance.

He told you this himself.

BERTRAM
And by other warranted testimony.

And I've heard from other sources.

LAFEU
Then my dial goes not true: I took this lark for a bunting.

Then my instincts were off: I thought this lark was a bunting.

BERTRAM
I do assure you, my lord, he is very great in knowledge and accordingly valiant.

I can promise you, my lord, he is very wise and his bravery matches it.

LAFEU
I have then sinned against his experience and transgressed against his valour; and my state that
way is dangerous, since I cannot yet find in my heart to repent. Here he comes: I pray you, make us friends; I will pursue the amity.

Then I have been unfair to his experience and wronged his bravery; and that makes my position perilous, since I can't find it in myself to apologise. Here he comes: please, make us friends; I'll do my part.

Enter PAROLLES

PAROLLES
[To BERTRAM] These things shall be done, sir.

These things shall be done, sir.

LAFEU
Pray you, sir, who's his tailor?

Now tell me sir, who's his tailor?

PAROLLES
Sir?

Sir?

LAFEU
O, I know him well, I, sir; he, sir, 's a good
workman, a very good tailor.

*Oh, I know him well, sir; he's a good
workman, sir, a very good tailor.*

BERTRAM
[Aside to PAROLLES] Is she gone to the king?

Has she gone to the King?

PAROLLES
She is.

She has.

BERTRAM
Will she away to-night?

Will she leave tonight?

PAROLLES
As you'll have her.

As you have ordered.

BERTRAM
I have writ my letters, casketed my treasure,
Given order for our horses; and to-night,
When I should take possession of the bride,
End ere I do begin.

*I have written my farewells, crated up my
valuables, ordered our horses; and tonight,
when I should be consummating my marriage
I'll be back where I started.*

LAFEU
A good traveller is something at the latter end of
a
dinner; but one that lies three thirds and uses a
known truth to pass a thousand nothings with,
should
be once heard and thrice beaten. God save you,
captain.

*A well travelled man can be entertaining at the
end
of dinner; but one who tells nothing but lies and
uses
one truth to backup a thousand fantasies should
be listened to once and beaten three times. God
bless you, captain.*

BERTRAM
Is there any unkindness between my lord and
you, monsieur?

*Is there any bad feeling between my lord and
you, sir?*

PAROLLES
I know not how I have deserved to run into my
lord's
displeasure.

*I don't know what I've done to deserve my lord's
disapproval.*

LAFEU
You have made shift to run into 't, boots and
spurs
and all, like him that leaped into the custard; and
out of it you'll run again, rather than suffer
question for your residence.

*You made an effort to run into it, boots and
spurs
and all, like the one who leaped into the
custard; and you will run out of it again, rather
than answer questions about why you are there.*

BERTRAM
It may be you have mistaken him, my lord.

Maybe you misunderstood him, my lord.

LAFEU
And shall do so ever, though I took him at 's
prayers. Fare you well, my lord; and believe this
of me, there can be no kernel in this light nut;
the
soul of this man is his clothes. Trust him not in
matter of heavy consequence; I have kept of
them
tame, and know their natures. Farewell,
monsieur:
I have spoken better of you than you have or
will to
deserve at my hand; but we must do good
against evil.

*And I always will do, even if I found him
praying. Farewell, my lord; and mark my words,
there is no heart to this fellow; his soul
is all his clothes. Don't trust him for
any important matters; I've kept men like this
as pets, and I know what they're like. Farewell,
monsieur:
I have spoken better of you than you deserve
from me;
but we must all do our best to be good.*

Exit

PAROLLES
An idle lord. I swear.

A useless lord, I swear

BERTRAM
I think so.

I think so.

PAROLLES
Why, do you not know him?

Why, don't you know him?

BERTRAM
Yes, I do know him well, and common speech
Gives him a worthy pass. Here comes my clog.

*Yes, I do know him well, and he has
a good reputation. Here is my ball and chain.*

Enter HELENA

HELENA
I have, sir, as I was commanded from you,
Spoke with the king and have procured his leave
For present parting; only he desires
Some private speech with you.

*Sir, as you have ordered I have
spoken with the King and got his permission
to leave at once; but he wants
to have a private word with you.*

BERTRAM
I shall obey his will.
You must not marvel, Helen, at my course,
Which holds not colour with the time, nor does

*I shall do as he asks.
You mustn't be surprised, Helen, at what I do,
which may not seem appropriate for the time*

The ministration and required office
On my particular. Prepared I was not
For such a business; therefore am I found
So much unsettled: this drives me to entreat you
That presently you take our way for home;
And rather muse than ask why I entreat you,
For my respects are better than they seem
And my appointments have in them a need
Greater than shows itself at the first view
To you that know them not. This to my mother:

Giving a letter

'Twill be two days ere I shall see you, so
I leave you to your wisdom.

HELENA
Sir, I can nothing say,
But that I am your most obedient servant.

BERTRAM
Come, come, no more of that.

HELENA
And ever shall
With true observance seek to eke out that
Wherein toward me my homely stars have fail'd
To equal my great fortune.

BERTRAM
Let that go:
My haste is very great: farewell; hie home.

HELENA
Pray, sir, your pardon.

BERTRAM
Well, what would you say?

HELENA
I am not worthy of the wealth I owe,
Nor dare I say 'tis mine, and yet it is;
But, like a timorous thief, most fain would steal
What law does vouch mine own.

BERTRAM

*and does not fit with me fulfilling
my obligations. I was not ready
for this business; so I am
rather in a whirl: so I'm asking you
to go home at once;
and you should wonder, rather than ask me, why
I ask you to do this, for I am being more
respectful than it might seem and my
appointments are more pressing than may
appear to you, knowing nothing about them.
Give this to my mother:*

*I will see you in two days,
until then I leave you to your own devices.*

*Sir, I can say nothing,
except that I am your most obedient servant.*

Now now, that's enough of that.

*And I shall always
try to behave properly to make up the
deficiencies of my humble birth, which does not
match my great fortune.*

*Never mind that:
I'm in a great hurry: farewell, hurry home.*

Excuse me, sir.

Well, what do you want to say?

*I do not deserve the riches I have got,
nor do I dare believe they're mine, but they are;
but, like a cowardly thief, I want to steal
my own property.*

What would you have?

What do you want?

HELENA
Something; and scarce so much: nothing,
indeed.
I would not tell you what I would, my lord:
Faith yes;
Strangers and foes do sunder, and not kiss.

Something; hardly anything: nothing in fact.
I won't tell you what I want, my lord:
actually I will;
strangers and enemies do not kiss when they
part.

BERTRAM
I pray you, stay not, but in haste to horse.

I'm telling you, don't stop here, hurry to your
horse.

HELENA
I shall not break your bidding, good my lord.

I shall follow your orders, my good lord.

BERTRAM
Where are my other men, monsieur? Farewell.

Where are my other men, sir? Farewell.

Exit HELENA

(Exit Helena)

Go thou toward home; where I will never come
Whilst I can shake my sword or hear the drum.
Away, and for our flight.

Go off home; the place I will never go
while I can still hold a sword or hear the drum.
Come on, let's make our escape.

PAROLLES
Bravely, coragio!

Bravely, with courage!

Exeunt

Act 3

SCENE I. Florence. The DUKE's palace.

Flourish. Enter the DUKE of Florence attended; the two Frenchmen, with a troop of soldiers.

DUKE
So that from point to point now have you heard
The fundamental reasons of this war,
Whose great decision hath much blood let forth
And more thirsts after.

*So you have now heard from start to finish
the principal reasons for this war,
which has caused so much blood to be spilt
and it seems there is more to come.*

First Lord
Holy seems the quarrel
Upon your grace's part; black and fearful
On the opposer.

*Your grace's reasons seem
justified; your enemy's seem
to be totally wrong.*

DUKE
Therefore we marvel much our cousin France
Would in so just a business shut his bosom
Against our borrowing prayers.

*That's why I'm so amazed that my French cousin
would close his ears, given how right we are,
to our pleas for help.*

Second Lord
Good my lord,
The reasons of our state I cannot yield,
But like a common and an outward man,
That the great figure of a council frames
By self-unable motion: therefore dare not
Say what I think of it, since I have found
Myself in my incertain grounds to fail
As often as I guess'd.

*My good lord,
I cannot argue against my country's policy,
I am just like an ordinary man,
and I am bound to follow the great decisions
of the Council: so I do not dare
to say what I think of it, because
my opinions are often wrong.*

DUKE
Be it his pleasure.

He must do what he thinks best.

First Lord
But I am sure the younger of our nature,
That surfeit on their ease, will day by day
Come here for physic.

*But I am sure that our younger men,
who become ill from too much leisure, will daily
come here for a cure.*

DUKE
Welcome shall they be;
And all the honours that can fly from us
Shall on them settle. You know your places
well;

*They shall be welcome;
and all the honours I have to give
will be theirs. You know your places;
when better men fall, they fell to make room for*

When better fall, for your avails they fell: *you:*
To-morrow to the field. *tomorrow we go to the battlefield.*

Flourish. Exeunt

SCENE II. Rousillon. The COUNT's palace.

Enter COUNTESS and Clown

COUNTESS
It hath happened all as I would have had it, save that he comes not along with her.

Everything has happened as I wanted, except that he has not come with her.

Clown
By my troth, I take my young lord to be a very melancholy man.

I swear, I think that my young lord is a very unhappy man.

COUNTESS
By what observance, I pray you?

And what makes you say this, may I ask?

Clown
Why, he will look upon his boot and sing; mend the
ruff and sing; ask questions and sing; pick his teeth and sing. I know a man that had this trick of
melancholy sold a goodly manor for a song.

*Well, when he looks at his boot he sings; he mends
his ruff and sings; asks questions and sings; picks his
teeth and sings. I knew a man with this sort of depression who sold a good estate for a song.*

COUNTESS
Let me see what he writes, and when he means to come.

Let me see what is written, and when he means to come here.

Opening a letter

Clown
I have no mind to Isbel since I was at court: our old ling and our Isbels o' the country are nothing like your old ling and your Isbels o' the court: the brains of my Cupid's knocked out, and I begin to
love, as an old man loves money, with no stomach.

*I haven't thought of Isbel since I was at the court: our old trouts and the Isbels of the country are nothingcompared to the old trouts and the Isbels at court:
my love has been murdered, and now I love with no appetite, the way an old man loves money.*

COUNTESS
What have we here?

What have we here?

Clown
E'en that you have there.

Whatever it is that you have there.

Exit

COUNTESS
[Reads] I have sent you a daughter-in-law: she hath
recovered the king, and undone me. I have wedded
her, not bedded her; and sworn to make the 'not' eternal. You shall hear I am run away: know it
before the report come. If there be breadth enough
in the world, I will hold a long distance. My duty
to you. Your unfortunate son,

BERTRAM.
This is not well, rash and unbridled boy.
To fly the favours of so good a king;
To pluck his indignation on thy head
By the misprising of a maid too virtuous
For the contempt of empire.

Re-enter Clown

Clown
O madam, yonder is heavy news within between two
soldiers and my young lady!

COUNTESS
What is the matter?

Clown
Nay, there is some comfort in the news, some comfort; your son will not be killed so soon as I thought he would.

COUNTESS
Why should he be killed?

Clown
So say I, madam, if he run away, as I hear he does:
the danger is in standing to't; that's the loss of men, though it be the getting of children. Here they come will tell you more: for my part, I only

*I have sent you a daughter-in-law; she has saved the King, and ruined me. I have married her,
not slept with her, and I don't intend that I ever should. You will hear that I have run away: this is
to let you know before you hear from someone else. If there is enough space
in the world I'll keep my distance. My respects
to you. Your unlucky son,*

*Bertram.
This is not good, you foolish headstrong boy.
You should not upset such a good king;
you will bring his anger down upon you
for misusing such a good girl
and for defying his authority.*

*Oh madam, there is bad news in there, brought by
two soldiers and my young lady!*

What's the matter?

Well, there is some good news, some comfort; your son will not be killed as quickly as I thought he would be.

Why would he be killed?

*I say the same, madam, if he runs away, as I hear he has:
the danger is in standing up; that's what brings men down, though it's how children are made. Here come the ones who can tell you more: as*

hear your son was run away.

Exit

Enter HELENA, and two Gentlemen

First Gentleman
Save you, good madam.

HELENA
Madam, my lord is gone, for ever gone.

Second Gentleman
Do not say so.

COUNTESS
Think upon patience. Pray you, gentlemen,
I have felt so many quirks of joy and grief,
That the first face of neither, on the start,
Can woman me unto't: where is my son, I pray
you?

Second Gentleman
Madam, he's gone to serve the duke of Florence:
We met him thitherward; for thence we came,
And, after some dispatch in hand at court,
Thither we bend again.

HELENA
Look on his letter, madam; here's my passport.
Reads
When thou canst get the ring upon my finger
which
never shall come off, and show me a child
begotten
of thy body that I am father to, then call me
husband: but in such a 'then' I write a 'never.'
This is a dreadful sentence.

COUNTESS
Brought you this letter, gentlemen?

First Gentleman
Ay, madam;
And for the contents' sake are sorry for our pain.

for me,
all I hear is that your son has run away.

Blessings on you, good lady.

Madam, my lord is gone, gone forever.

Don't say so.

Be patient. Please gentlemen,
I have felt so many twists of joy and grief,
that I do not know which one
to believe: please tell me, where is my son?

Madam, he's gone to serve the Duke of
Florence: we met him on his way there: for
that's where we came from,
and, after delivering our messages at the court
we're going back there.

Look at his letter, madam; this is my dismissal.
(reads)
When you can put a ring on my finger which
I can't take off, and show me a child from
your womb that I am the father of, then you can
call me
husband: but I tell you such a thing will never
happen.
This is terrible sentence.

Did you bring this letter, gentlemen?

Yes, madam;
and now we hear it we're sorry we did.

COUNTESS
I prithee, lady, have a better cheer;
If thou engrossest all the griefs are thine,
Thou robb'st me of a moiety: he was my son;
But I do wash his name out of my blood,
And thou art all my child. Towards Florence is
he?

Please, lady, be more cheerful;
if you take all the grief for yourself,
you will rob me of my share: he was my son;
but I disown him
and you are my only child. He's going to
Florence is he?

Second Gentleman
Ay, madam.

Yes, madam.

COUNTESS
And to be a soldier?

To be a soldier?

Second Gentleman
Such is his noble purpose; and believe 't,
The duke will lay upon him all the honour
That good convenience claims.

That is his noble purpose; and I assure you
the Duke will give him all the honor
available to him.

COUNTESS
Return you thither?

Are you going back there?

First Gentleman
Ay, madam, with the swiftest wing of speed.

Yes madam, as quick as we can.

HELENA
[Reads] Till I have no wife I have nothing in
France.
'Tis bitter.

[Reading] Until I have no wife there's nothing
for me in France.
That's bitter.

COUNTESS
Find you that there?

Is that what it says?

HELENA
Ay, madam.

Yes, madam.

First Gentleman
'Tis but the boldness of his hand, haply, which
his
heart was not consenting to.

Maybe these are just rash words, which he
didn't really mean.

COUNTESS
Nothing in France, until he have no wife!
There's nothing here that is too good for him
But only she; and she deserves a lord
That twenty such rude boys might tend upon

There's nothing in France, until he has no wife!
The only thing here that is too good for him
is her; she deserves a lord who has
Twenty rude boys like him as servants

And call her hourly mistress. Who was with
him?

First Gentleman
A servant only, and a gentleman
Which I have sometime known.

COUNTESS
Parolles, was it not?

First Gentleman
Ay, my good lady, he.

COUNTESS
A very tainted fellow, and full of wickedness.
My son corrupts a well-derived nature
With his inducement.

First Gentleman
Indeed, good lady,
The fellow has a deal of that too much,
Which holds him much to have.

COUNTESS
You're welcome, gentlemen.
I will entreat you, when you see my son,
To tell him that his sword can never win
The honour that he loses: more I'll entreat you
Written to bear along.

Second Gentleman
We serve you, madam,
In that and all your worthiest affairs.

COUNTESS
Not so, but as we change our courtesies.
Will you draw near!

Exeunt COUNTESS and Gentlemen

HELENA
'Till I have no wife, I have nothing in France.'
Nothing in France, until he has no wife!
Thou shalt have none, Rousillon, none in
France;

*who would call her mistress every hour. Who
was with him?*

*Just a servant, and a gentleman
I have met before.*

Parolles, wasn't it?

Yes, my good lady, it was him.

*A very bad character, full of wickedness.
He has persuaded my son to go against
his good nature.*

*Indeed, good lady,
the fellow has far too much
of things he shouldn't have.*

*Gentlemen, you are welcome.
I beg you, when you see my son,
tell him that he can never win with his sword
the honour that he is losing: and what's more I'll
ask that you take a letter to him.*

*We are at your service, madam,
in this and in all your noble business.*

*It's not the case, but your courtesy is
appreciated. Will you come with me!*

*'Until I have no wife, there's nothing for me in
France.'
Nothing in France, in till he has no wife!
You shall have none, Rousillon, none in France;*

Then hast thou all again. Poor lord! is't I
That chase thee from thy country and expose
Those tender limbs of thine to the event
Of the none-sparing war? and is it I
That drive thee from the sportive court, where thou
Wast shot at with fair eyes, to be the mark
Of smoky muskets? O you leaden messengers,
That ride upon the violent speed of fire,
Fly with false aim; move the still-peering air,
That sings with piercing; do not touch my lord.

Whoever shoots at him, I set him there;
Whoever charges on his forward breast,
I am the caitiff that do hold him to't;
And, though I kill him not, I am the cause
His death was so effected: better 'twere
I met the ravin lion when he roar'd
With sharp constraint of hunger; better 'twere
That all the miseries which nature owes
Were mine at once. No, come thou home, Rousillon,
Whence honour but of danger wins a scar,
As oft it loses all: I will be gone;
My being here it is that holds thee hence:
Shall I stay here to do't? no, no, although
The air of paradise did fan the house
And angels officed all: I will be gone,
That pitiful rumour may report my flight,
To consolate thine ear. Come, night; end, day!
For with the dark, poor thief, I'll steal away.

Exit

*then you will get everything back. Poor lord! Is
it I who chases you from your country and
exposes those young limbs of yours to the risk
of the all consuming war? And is it I
who chases you from the jolly court, where you
were shot at with glances from fair eyes, to be
the target of smoking rifles? Oh you messengers
of lead, thatare pushed along by the violence of
explosions,
be badly aimed; fly through the empty air
that sings with your noise; do not touch my lord.*

*Whoever shoots at him, I put him there;
whoever charges towards his chest,
I am the coward that put him in the firing line;
and although I do not kill him, I will be the
reason for his death: it would be better
if I faced a raging lion, roaring
in his hunger; it would be better
if all the miseries of the world
became mine at once. No, come home,
Rousillon,
from where honor may get a scar from danger,
but just as often loses everything: I will go;
my being here is all that keeps you away:
will I stay here to keep you out? No, no, not
even if this house was in paradise
with angels for servants: I will go,
so that the gossip can report my flight
and make you feel better. Come, night; end, day!
I will disappear like a poor thief in the night.*

SCENE III. Florence. Before the DUKE's palace.

Flourish. Enter the DUKE of Florence, BERTRAM, PAROLLES, Soldiers, Drum, and Trumpets

DUKE
The general of our horse thou art; and we,
Great in our hope, lay our best love and credence
Upon thy promising fortune.

*You are the leader of our cavalry; and I
have great hopes of you, and am putting my faith and belief
in your promising talents.*

BERTRAM
Sir, it is
A charge too heavy for my strength, but yet
We'll strive to bear it for your worthy sake
To the extreme edge of hazard.

*Sir, it is
too much responsibility for me, but still
for your worthy sake we will do our best
to the utmost extreme.*

DUKE
Then go thou forth;
And fortune play upon thy prosperous helm,
As thy auspicious mistress!

*Then go into battle;
and may luck shine upon your helmet,
as your happy mistress!*

BERTRAM
This very day,
Great Mars, I put myself into thy file:
Make me but like my thoughts, and I shall prove
A lover of thy drum, hater of love.

*This is the day,
great Mars, that I join your ranks:
if my actions follow my thoughts I will show myself
a lover of your drum, a hater of love.*

Exeunt

SCENE IV. Rousillon. The COUNT's palace.

Enter COUNTESS and Steward

COUNTESS
Alas! and would you take the letter of her?
Might you not know she would do as she has
done, By sending me a letter? Read it again.

*Alas! Why did you accept a letter from her?
Couldn't you guess that she would do what she
has done,
by sending me a letter? Read it again.*

Steward
[Reads] I am Saint Jaques' pilgrim, thither gone:
Ambitious love hath so in me offended, That
barefoot plod I the cold ground upon, With
sainted vow my faults to have amended. Write,
write, that from the bloody course of war My
dearest master, your dear son, may hie: Bless
him at home in peace, whilst I from far His
name with zealous fervor sanctify: His taken
labours bid him me forgive; I, his despiteful
Juno, sent him forth From courtly friends, with
camping foes to live, Where death and danger
dogs the heels of worth: He is too good and fair
for death and me: Whom I myself embrace, to
set him free.

*I have gone on a pilgrimage to St James:
my ambitious love has caused such offence
that I am going to walk the cold ground
barefoot, asking the saint to correct my
thoughts. Please write to my dearest master,
your dear son, so that he will come back from
the bloody war; give him peace at home, while I
from far off will worship his name passionately:
ask him to forgive me the trouble I have caused
him; I, like a spiteful goddess, have sent him
away from his friends at court, to live with his
encamped enemies, where death and danger
hunts down the noble: he is too good and too
beautiful for death and for me: I embrace death
myself, so that he can be free.*

COUNTESS
Ah, what sharp stings are in her mildest words!
Rinaldo, you did never lack advice so much, As
letting her pass so: had I spoke with her, I could
have well diverted her intents, Which thus she
hath prevented.

*Ah, her humble words are like daggers!
Rinaldo, you never did such an unwise thing
as letting her go like this: if I'd spoken to her
I could easily have put her off,
but with this letter she has avoided that.*

Steward
Pardon me, madam: If I had given you this at
over-night, She might have been o'erta'en; and
yet she writes, Pursuit would be but vain.

*Please excuse me, madam: if I had woken you
with this she might have been overtaken: and
yet, as she writes, it would be pointless to chase
her.*

COUNTESS
What angel shall
Bless this unworthy husband? he cannot thrive,
Unless her prayers, whom heaven delights to
hear
And loves to grant, reprieve him from the wrath
Of greatest justice. Write, write, Rinaldo,
To this unworthy husband of his wife;

*What angel will
give a blessing to this unworthy husband? He
cannot do well unless her prayers, from one
heaven loves to hear from
and answer, save him from the anger
of divine justice. Write, write, Rinaldo,
to this unworthy husband about his wife;*

Let every word weigh heavy of her worth
That he does weigh too light: my greatest grief.
Though little he do feel it, set down sharply.
Dispatch the most convenient messenger:
When haply he shall hear that she is gone,
He will return; and hope I may that she,
Hearing so much, will speed her foot again,
Led hither by pure love: which of them both
Is dearest to me. I have no skill in sense
To make distinction: provide this messenger:
My heart is heavy and mine age is weak;
Grief would have tears, and sorrow bids me
speak.

Exeunt

*let every word show him her value
which he regards too cheaply: show my great
grief. However little he feels it, force him to.
Send the best messenger:
hopefully when he hears that she is gone
he will come back; and I hope maybe that she,
hearing that he has, will rush back here,
led by pure love: both of them
are equally dear to me. I don't have the ability
to distinguish between the two: get the
messenger: my heart is heavy and old age makes
me weak; grief wants me to cry, and sorrow
makes me speak.*

SCENE V. Florence. Without the walls. A tucket afar off.

Enter an old Widow of Florence, DIANA, VIOLENTA, and MARIANA, with other Citizens

Widow
Nay, come; for if they do approach the city, we
shall lose all the sight.

Come on; if they come to the city, we will miss seeing them.

DIANA
They say the French count has done most
honourable service.

They say the French count has done great service.

Widow
It is reported that he has taken their greatest
commander; and that with his own hand he slew
the
duke's brother.

*It is reported that he captured their greatest commander; and that he killed the Duke's brother
with his own hand.*

Tucket

(Trumpet)

We have lost our labour; they are gone a
contrary
way: hark! you may know by their trumpets.

We have wasted our time, they have gone round another way: listen! You can hear their trumpets.

MARIANA
Come, let's return again, and suffice ourselves
with
the report of it. Well, Diana, take heed of this
French earl: the honour of a maid is her name;
and
no legacy is so rich as honesty.

*Come on, let's go back, and be happy with hearing the report. Well, Diana, make a note of this
French earl: a maid has her honor as her fame; and
honesty is greater than any inheritance.*

Widow
I have told my neighbour how you have been
solicited
by a gentleman his companion.

*I was telling my neighbour how you have been propositioned
by a gentleman who is his companion.*

MARIANA
I know that knave; hang him! one Parolles: a
filthy officer he is in those suggestions for the
young earl. Beware of them, Diana; their
promises,
enticements, oaths, tokens, and all these engines
of

*I know that knave; hang him! He's called Parolles: he
is a filthy officer, making those suggestions for the
young Earl. Be wary of them, Diana; their promises,*

lust, are not the things they go under: many a
maid
hath been seduced by them; and the misery is,
example, that so terrible shows in the wreck of
maidenhood, cannot for all that dissuade
succession,
but that they are limed with the twigs that
threaten
them. I hope I need not to advise you further;
but
I hope your own grace will keep you where you
are,
though there were no further danger known but
the
modesty which is so lost.

bribes, oaths, presents, and all the other
machinery of
lust, are not things they take seriously: many
maids
have been seduced by them; and the terrible
thing is,
that all these examples, which show how awful
the loss
of virginity is, still cannot stop them from falling
and being caught in the traps that are set for
them.
I hope I don't need to give you any other advice;
I hope your own grace will keep you where you
are,
even if the only danger was a loss of modesty.

DIANA
You shall not need to fear me.

You don't need to worry about me.

Widow
I hope so.

I hope so.

Enter HELENA, disguised like a Pilgrim

Look, here comes a pilgrim: I know she will lie
at
my house; thither they send one another: I'll
question her. God save you, pilgrim! whither are
you bound?

Look, here comes a pilgrim: I know she will rest
at
my house; they send each other there: I'll
question her. God bless you, pilgrim! Where are
you going?

HELENA
To Saint Jaques le Grand.
Where do the palmers lodge, I do beseech you?

To great St James.
Please can you tell me where the Pilgrims stay?

Widow
At the Saint Francis here beside the port.

At the St Francis here by the port.

HELENA
Is this the way?

Is this the way?

Widow
Ay, marry, is't.

That's right.

A march afar

Hark you! they come this way.
If you will tarry, holy pilgrim,
But till the troops come by,
I will conduct you where you shall be lodged;
The rather, for I think I know your hostess
As ample as myself.

Listen! There are coming this way.
If you will wait, holy pilgrim,
just until the troops have passed,
I will take you to your lodging;
I'll be pleased to, for I think I know your hostess
as well as I know myself.

HELENA
Is it yourself?

Is it you?

Widow
If you shall please so, pilgrim.

If you will accept, pilgrim.

HELENA
I thank you, and will stay upon your leisure.

I thank you, and will wait until you are ready.

Widow
You came, I think, from France?

You came from France I think?

HELENA
I did so.

I did.

Widow
Here you shall see a countryman of yours
That has done worthy service.

You shall see a countryman of yours here
who has done good service.

HELENA
His name, I pray you.

Please tell me his name.

DIANA
The Count Rousillon: know you such a one?

The Count Rousillon: do you know him?

HELENA
But by the ear, that hears most nobly of him:
His face I know not.

Only by reputation, which is very good:
I don't know his face.

DIANA
Whatsome'er he is,
He's bravely taken here. He stole from France,
As 'tis reported, for the king had married him
Against his liking: think you it is so?

Whatever he may be,
he's done well here. He sneaked away from
France, so they say, because the king had made
him marry
against his will: do you think that's true?

HELENA
Ay, surely, mere the truth: I know his lady.

Yes, that's nothing but the truth: I know his lady.

DIANA

There is a gentleman that serves the count
Reports but coarsely of her.

HELENA
What's his name?

DIANA
Monsieur Parolles.

HELENA
O, I believe with him,
In argument of praise, or to the worth
Of the great count, she is too mean
To have her name repeated: all her deserving
Is a reserved honesty, and that
I have not heard examined.

DIANA
Alas, poor lady!
'Tis a hard bondage to become the wife
Of a detesting lord.

Widow
I warrant, good creature, wheresoe'er she is,
Her heart weighs sadly: this young maid might do her
A shrewd turn, if she pleased.

HELENA
How do you mean?
May be the amorous count solicits her
In the unlawful purpose.

Widow
He does indeed;
And brokes with all that can in such a suit
Corrupt the tender honour of a maid:
But she is arm'd for him and keeps her guard
In honestest defence.

MARIANA
The gods forbid else!

Widow
So, now they come:

The count has a gentleman attending him who only has bad things to say about her.

What's his name?

Monsieur Parolles.

Oh, I think for him or for the great count himself, she is too low to be praised or even have her name spoken: her only virtue is her quiet honesty, and I haven't heard anybody question that.

Alas, poor lady! It's thankless task to be the wife of a husband who hates you.

I'll bet that the good creature, wherever she is, has a heavy heart: this young maid might do her a good turn, if she wished.

How do you mean? Maybe the randy count is paying attention to her from impure motives.

He is indeed; and has been throwing everything at her that could corrupt the tender honour of a maid.

Heaven forbid!

Look, they're coming:

Drum and Colours

Enter BERTRAM, PAROLLES, and the whole army

That is Antonio, the duke's eldest son;
That, Escalus.

That is Antonio, the Duke's eldest son;
that one is Escalus.

HELENA
Which is the Frenchman?

Which one is the Frenchman?

DIANA
He;
That with the plume: 'tis a most gallant fellow.
I would he loved his wife: if he were honester
He were much goodlier: is't not a handsome
gentleman?

That one;
the one with the plume: he is a brave chap.
I wish he loved his wife: if he were more honest
he would be a better man: isn't he handsome?

HELENA
I like him well.

I like him very much.

DIANA
'Tis pity he is not honest: yond's that same knave
That leads him to these places: were I his lady,
I would Poison that vile rascal.

It's a pity he's not honest: over there is the knave
who makes him do these things: if I were his
wife I would poison that foul scoundrel.

HELENA
Which is he?

Which one is he?

DIANA
That jack-an-apes with scarfs: why is he
melancholy?

That monkey with the scarves: why does he look
sad?

HELENA
Perchance he's hurt i' the battle.

Maybe he's been hurt in the battle.

PAROLLES
Lose our drum! well.

We've lost our drum! Well.

MARIANA
He's shrewdly vexed at something: look, he has
spied us.

He's definitely annoyed about something: look,
he's spotted us.

Widow
Marry, hang you!

Ah, hang you!

MARIANA

And your courtesy, for a ring-carrier! *And your politeness as a pimp!*

Exeunt BERTRAM, PAROLLES, and army

Widow
The troop is past. Come, pilgrim, I will bring
you
Where you shall host: of enjoin'd penitents
There's four or five, to great Saint Jaques bound,
Already at my house.

*The parade is over. Come on, pilgrim, I will
bring you
to your lodgings. there are already four or five
sworn Pilgrims, headed for great St James.
at my house.*

HELENA
I humbly thank you:
Please it this matron and this gentle maid
To eat with us to-night, the charge and thanking
Shall be for me; and, to requite you further,
I will bestow some precepts of this virgin
Worthy the note.

*I give you my humble thanks.
if you are agreeable I would like this lady and
this gentle girl
to eat with us tonight, at my expense
and for my pleasure; and, to pay you further,
I will give you some advice
that will be worth listening to.*

BOTH
We'll take your offer kindly. *We'd be glad to accept.*

Exeunt

SCENE VI. Camp before Florence.

Enter BERTRAM and the two French Lords

Second Lord
Nay, good my lord, put him to't; let him have his
way.

No, my good lord, put him to the test; see what he does.

First Lord
If your lordship find him not a hilding, hold me
no
more in your respect.

*If your lordship doesn't find that he's a coward, have no respect
for me any more.*

Second Lord
On my life, my lord, a bubble.

I swear on my life, my lord, he's a coward.

BERTRAM
Do you think I am so far deceived in him?

Do you think I could be so much mistaken?

Second Lord
Believe it, my lord, in mine own direct
knowledge,
without any malice, but to speak of him as my
kinsman, he's a most notable coward, an infinite
and
endless liar, an hourly promise-breaker, the
owner
of no one good quality worthy your lordship's
entertainment.

*You should believe it, my lord, I have seen it myself,
I'm not speaking with any malice, but speaking of him as my
kinsman, he's a complete coward, he never stops lying,
breaks promises every hour, and has not a single
good quality to recommend him to you.*

First Lord
It were fit you knew him; lest, reposing too far
in
his virtue, which he hath not, he might at some
great and trusty business in a main danger fail
you.

*It's best that you know what he's like, in case you put too much trust
in his goodness, of which he has none, and then he might
fail you in some great important business.*

BERTRAM
I would I knew in what particular action to try
him.

I wish I knew the best way to test him.

First Lord
None better than to let him fetch off his drum,
which you hear him so confidently undertake to
do.

No better way than to tell him to get his drum, which you've heard him so confidently say he will do.

Second Lord
I, with a troop of Florentines, will suddenly
surprise him; such I will have, whom I am sure
he
knows not from the enemy: we will bind and
hoodwink
him so, that he shall suppose no other but that he
is carried into the leaguer of the adversaries,
when
we bring him to our own tents. Be but your
lordship
present at his examination: if he do not, for the
promise of his life and in the highest compulsion
of
base fear, offer to betray you and deliver all the
intelligence in his power against you, and that
with
the divine forfeit of his soul upon oath, never
trust my judgment in any thing.

*I, with a troop of Florentines, will suddenly
ambush him; I have some whom I'm sure he
doesn't know from the enemy: we will try and
blindfold
him so that he thinks that he has been carried
into a meeting of the enemy, when
we bring him into our own tents. All you have to
do
is be present when we question him: if he does
not,
in return for his life and out of cowardice,
offer to betray you and gives up all the secrets
he has that could harm you, swearing that
they are true with a holy oath, never
trust my judgement again.*

First Lord
O, for the love of laughter, let him fetch his
drum;
he says he has a stratagem for't: when your
lordship sees the bottom of his success in't, and
to
what metal this counterfeit lump of ore will be
melted, if you give him not John Drum's
entertainment, your inclining cannot be
removed.
Here he comes.

*Oh, for the fun of it, tell him to fetch his drum;
he says he has a plan for it: when your lordship
sees what this will lead to, and to
what base metal this fake lump of ore will be
reduced to, if you don't play this game
with the drum, you will always have doubts.
Here he comes.*

Enter PAROLLES

Second Lord
[Aside to BERTRAM] O, for the love of
laughter,
hinder not the honour of his design: let him
fetch
off his drum in any hand.

*Oh, for the sake of fun,
do not block him in his plan: let him go
and get his drum in any way he wants.*

BERTRAM
How now, monsieur! this drum sticks sorely in
your
disposition.

*How are you, sir! I can see this business of the
drum
is bothering you.*

First Lord

A pox on't, let it go; 'tis but a drum.

Blast the thing man, let it go; it's only a drum.

PAROLLES

'But a drum'! is't 'but a drum'? A drum so lost!
There was excellent command,--to charge in with our
horse upon our own wings, and to rend our own soldiers!

'Only a drum'! Is it ' only a drum'? A drum lost like that!
There was an excellent command-to charge with our cavalry against our own wings, and to tear into our own soldiers!

First Lord

That was not to be blamed in the command of the
service: it was a disaster of war that Caesar
himself could not have prevented, if he had been there to command.

That was not the fault of the commander: it was a disaster of war that Caesar himself could not have prevented, if he had been in command.

BERTRAM

Well, we cannot greatly condemn our success: some
dishonour we had in the loss of that drum; but it is
not to be recovered.

Well, we mustn't let it spoil our victory: there was some dishonor for us in the loss of the drum, but we can't get it back.

PAROLLES

It might have been recovered.

We could have got it back.

BERTRAM

It might; but it is not now.

Could have, but can't now.

PAROLLES

It is to be recovered: but that the merit of
service is seldom attributed to the true and exact
performer, I would have that drum or another, or 'hic jacet.'

It can be got back: except for the fact that the credit is not often given to the one who deserves it, I would get that drum back or get another, or die here.

BERTRAM

Why, if you have a stomach, to't, monsieur: if you
think your mystery in stratagem can bring this
instrument of honour again into his native quarter,
be magnanimous in the enterprise and go on; I will
grace the attempt for a worthy exploit: if you
speed well in it, the duke shall both speak of it.

Why, if you have the guts for it, sir: if you think that your cunning can bring this symbol of honor back home again, then by all means follow your plan; I will honor the attempt as a noble deed: if you perform it well, the Duke shall not only speak of and extend to you what further becomes his greatness, even to the utmost syllable of your worthiness.

it;
he will offer you everything in his power
that you deserve.

PAROLLES
By the hand of a soldier, I will undertake it.

With a soldier's hand, I shall try.

BERTRAM
But you must not now slumber in it.

But you mustn't be slow about it.

PAROLLES
I'll about it this evening: and I will presently pen down my dilemmas, encourage myself in my
certainty, put myself into my mortal preparation; and by midnight look to hear further from me.

I'll get going this evening: I will shortly
write down the problems, build up my
belief, prepare my soul the death;
expect to hear more from me by midnight.

BERTRAM
May I be bold to acquaint his grace you are gone about it?

May I tell his grace that you're doing it?

PAROLLES
I know not what the success will be, my lord; but
the attempt I vow.

I don't know how successful I will be, my lord;
but
I promise I shall try.

BERTRAM
I know thou'rt valiant; and, to the possibility of thy soldiership, will subscribe for thee. Farewell.

I know that you're brave; and I will speak of you
with faith in your soldiership. Farewell.

PAROLLES
I love not many words.

I'm not a man who likes to use many words.

Exit

Second Lord
No more than a fish loves water. Is not this a strange fellow, my lord, that so confidently seems
to undertake this business, which he knows is not to
be done; damns himself to do and dares better be
damned than to do't?

No more so than a fish likes water. Isn't this
a strange fellow, my lord, who seems so
confident
that he can pull off this business, when he knows
it can't be done; he says may he be damned if he
doesn't.
do it, but he'd rather be damned than do it?

First Lord

You do not know him, my lord, as we do:
certain it
is that he will steal himself into a man's favour
and
for a week escape a great deal of discoveries;
but
when you find him out, you have him ever after.

*You do not know him, my lord, as we do: he can
definitely
get himself into a man's favor and for a week
he can avoid being found out; but
when you do find out about him you'll always
know him after that.*

BERTRAM

Why, do you think he will make no deed at all
of
this that so seriously he does address himself
unto?

*What, do you think he won't even try to do
this thing he's made such a show of promising?*

Second Lord

None in the world; but return with an invention
and
clap upon you two or three probable lies: but we
have almost embossed him; you shall see his fall
to-night; for indeed he is not for your lordship's
respect.

*There's not a chance in the world; he'll come
back with a story
and give you two or three believable lies: but we
have almost trapped him; you shall see his fall
tonight; for he certainly is not worthy of your
lordship's trust.*

First Lord

We'll make you some sport with the fox ere we
case
him. He was first smoked by the old lord Lafeu:
when his disguise and he is parted, tell me what
a
sprat you shall find him; which you shall see
this
very night.

*We'll have some fun with the fox before we cage
him. He was first found out by the old lord
Lafeu:
when his disguise is stripped off, you can tell me
how contemptible you find him; you shall see
this
tonight.*

Second Lord

I must go look my twigs: he shall be caught.

*I must go and set up my traps: we shall catch
him.*

BERTRAM

Your brother he shall go along with me.

Your brother will come along with me.

Second Lord

As't please your lordship: I'll leave you.

As your lordship wishes: I'll leave you.

Exit

BERTRAM

Now will I lead you to the house, and show you

Now I will take you to the house, and show you

The lass I spoke of.

that girl I spoke of.

First Lord
But you say she's honest.

But you say she's honest.

BERTRAM
That's all the fault: I spoke with her but once
And found her wondrous cold; but I sent to her,
By this same coxcomb that we have i' the wind,
Tokens and letters which she did re-send;
And this is all I have done. She's a fair creature:
Will you go see her?

That's the problem: I only spoke to her once
and found her very cold; but I sent her,
via this same fop that we have on our line,
presents and letters which she sent back;
this is all I have done. She's a lovely creature;
will you go and see her?

First Lord
With all my heart, my lord.

I certainly shall, my lord.

Exeunt

SCENE VII. Florence. The Widow's house

Enter HELENA and Widow

HELENA
If you misdoubt me that I am not she,
I know not how I shall assure you further,
But I shall lose the grounds I work upon.

If you doubt that I am her,
I don't know what else I can tell you,
and it will spoil my plans.

Widow
Though my estate be fallen, I was well born,
Nothing acquainted with these businesses;
And would not put my reputation now
In any staining act.

Although I am now humble, I was nobly born,
and don't know anything about this sort of thing;
and I would not risk my reputation now
by getting involved with anything dubious.

HELENA
Nor would I wish you.
First, give me trust, the count he is my husband,
And what to your sworn counsel I have spoken
Is so from word to word; and then you cannot,
By the good aid that I of you shall borrow,
Err in bestowing it.

And I wouldn't want you to.
Firstly, you must believe me, the count is my
husband, and the things I have told you under
oath are true from start to finish; if you believe
me then you will not be mistaken
in giving me your help.

Widow
I should believe you:
For you have show'd me that which well
approves
You're great in fortune.

I should believe you:
you have shown me proof that
you have a great fortune.

HELENA
Take this purse of gold,
And let me buy your friendly help thus far,
Which I will over-pay and pay again
When I have found it. The count he wooes your
daughter,
Lays down his wanton siege before her beauty,
Resolved to carry her: let her in fine consent,
As we'll direct her how 'tis best to bear it.
Now his important blood will nought deny
That she'll demand: a ring the county wears,
That downward hath succeeded in his house
From son to son, some four or five descents
Since the first father wore it: this ring he holds
In most rich choice; yet in his idle fire,
To buy his will, it would not seem too dear,

Take this purse of gold,
as a down payment for your help so far,
and I will double it, treble it,
when you help me more. The count is wooing
your daughter,
he is laying a lustful siege to her beauty,
he's determined to have her: let her pretend to
give in in the way that we direct her is best.
Now his hot blood will not deny her
anything she asks: there is a ring he wears
that has been handed down in his family from
father to son, for four or five generations since
the first one had it: it is very precious to him;
but in his heat he will not think it is too much to
get what he wants

Howe'er repented after.

however much he regrets it afterwards.

Widow
Now I see
The bottom of your purpose.

Now I see
what you're planning.

HELENA
You see it lawful, then: it is no more,
But that your daughter, ere she seems as won,
Desires this ring; appoints him an encounter;
In fine, delivers me to fill the time,
Herself most chastely absent: after this,
To marry her, I'll add three thousand crowns
To what is passed already.

You see it is lawful, then: all I want
is for your daughter, pretending she has given
in, to ask for this ring: she should arrange a
meeting with him, at which I will take her place,
she will be chastely absent: after this,
I'll add three thousand crowns to her dowry
to go with what I've already paid.

Widow
I have yielded:
Instruct my daughter how she shall persever,
That time and place with this deceit so lawful
May prove coherent. Every night he comes
With musics of all sorts and songs composed
To her unworthiness: it nothing steads us
To chide him from our eaves; for he persists
As if his life lay on't.

I agree:
tell my daughter how to behave,
so that this lawful deception
looks genuine. He comes here every night
with all sorts of musicians and songs written
to try and persuade her: it doesn't do any good
to berate him from our windows; he carries on
as if his life depended on it.

HELENA
Why then to-night
Let us assay our plot; which, if it speed,
Is wicked meaning in a lawful deed
And lawful meaning in a lawful act,
Where both not sin, and yet a sinful fact:
But let's about it.

Why then, tonight
let us try our plot; if it works
it means the lawful deed will be wickedly done
a lawful act will have lawful meaning,
neither of us will be sinning, yet the fact will be
sinful:
but let's get on with it.

Exeunt

Act 4

SCENE I. Without the Florentine camp.

Enter Second French Lord, with five or six other Soldiers in ambush

Second Lord
He can come no other way but by this hedge-
corner.
When you sally upon him, speak what terrible
language you will: though you understand it not
yourselves, no matter; for we must not seem to
understand him, unless some one among us
whom we
must produce for an interpreter.

First Soldier
Good captain, let me be the interpreter.

Second Lord
Art not acquainted with him? knows he not thy
voice?

First Soldier
No, sir, I warrant you.

Second Lord
But what linsey-woolsey hast thou to speak to us
again?

First Soldier
E'en such as you speak to me.

Second Lord
He must think us some band of strangers i' the
adversary's entertainment. Now he hath a smack
of
all neighbouring languages; therefore we must
every
one be a man of his own fancy, not to know
what we
speak one to another; so we seem to know, is to
know straight our purpose: choughs' language,
gabble enough, and good enough. As for you,
interpreter, you must seem very politic. But
couch,

He can only come round this corner of the
hedge.
When you ambush him, speak whatever
nonsense
you want: it doesn't matter if you don't
understand it; the important thing is that we
look like
we don't understand him, unless we produce
someone as an interpreter.

Good captain, let me be the interpreter.

You don't know him? He doesn't know your
voice?

I promise you he doesn't, sir.

But what gibberish will you use when you speak
to us?

The same as you speak to me.

He must believe that we are a group of
foreigners in the pay of the enemy. Now, he has
a smattering of the languages around here; and
so we must all
make up our own language, not knowing
what we are saying to each other; all that
matters is
that we look as if we understand: the twittering
of birds,
gabbling nonsense, will be good enough. As for
you,
interpreter, you mustseem very wise. But hush,

ho! here he comes, to beguile two hours in a
sleep,
and then to return and swear the lies he forges.

*look! He comes, planning to get a couple of
hours' sleep,
and then go back and swear to the lies he makes
up.*

Enter PAROLLES

PAROLLES
Ten o'clock: within these three hours 'twill be
time enough to go home. What shall I say I have
done? It must be a very plausive invention that
carries it: they begin to smoke me; and disgraces
have of late knocked too often at my door. I find
my tongue is too foolhardy; but my heart hath
the
fear of Mars before it and of his creatures, not
daring the reports of my tongue.

*Ten o'clock: if I stop about three hours then it
will be
time to go home. What shall I say I have
done? It must be a very plausible invention to
carry it off, they're beginning to suspect me; and
recently I've been involved in too many close
shaves. I find that I speak too much; but my
heart is afraid of war and everything to do with
it, not of what my tongue might say.*

Second Lord
This is the first truth that e'er thine own tongue
was guilty of.

*This is the first time your tongue ever told the
truth.*

PAROLLES
What the devil should move me to undertake the
recovery of this drum, being not ignorant of the
impossibility, and knowing I had no such
purpose? I
must give myself some hurts, and say I got them
in
exploit: yet slight ones will not carry it; they
will say, 'Came you off with so little?' and great
ones I dare not give. Wherefore, what's the
instance? Tongue, I must put you into a
butter-woman's mouth and buy myself another
of
Bajazet's mule, if you prattle me into these
perils.

*Why on earth did I say that I would
get this drum back, knowing that it was
impossible, and knowing I had no intention of
doing so?
I must give myself some wounds, and say I got
them
in the adventure: but small ones won't do; they
will say, 'how did you get away with that?' and
I'm not going to give myself large ones. So, what
evidence will I have? Tongue, I must give you to
a gossip and buy myself another from
from Balaam's ass, if you keep talking me into
such danger.*

Second Lord
Is it possible he should know what he is, and be
that he is?

*Can he really know what sort of person he is,
and still be like this?*

PAROLLES
I would the cutting of my garments would serve
the
turn, or the breaking of my Spanish sword.

*I wish that just cutting my clothes would be
enough,
or breaking my Spanish sword.*

Second Lord
We cannot afford you so.

We won't give you that much.

PAROLLES
Or the baring of my beard; and to say it was in
stratagem.

*Or I could shave my beard, and say it was
part of my plan.*

Second Lord
'Twould not do.

That wouldn't fool us.

PAROLLES
Or to drown my clothes, and say I was stripped.

*Or I could throw my clothes in the river, and say
I was stripped.*

Second Lord
Hardly serve.

That won't work.

PAROLLES
Though I swore I leaped from the window of the
citadel.

*And I could swear I jumped out of the castle
window.*

Second Lord
How deep?

From what height?

PAROLLES
Thirty fathom.

Two hundredfeet.

Second Lord
Three great oaths would scarce make that be
believed.

*You could swear that in triplicate and it would
hardly be believed.*

PAROLLES
I would I had any drum of the enemy's: I would
swear
I recovered it.

*I wish I had a drum of the enemy's: I would
swear
that I had recovered it.*

Second Lord
You shall hear one anon.

You'll be hearing one soon.

PAROLLES
A drum now of the enemy's,--

Now, a drum of the enemy's-

Alarum within

Second Lord
Throca movousus, cargo, cargo, cargo.

Throca movousus, cargo, cargo, cargo.

All

First Soldier

Cargo, cargo, cargo, villiando par corbo, cargo.

PAROLLES
O, ransom, ransom! do not hide mine eyes.

They seize and blindfold him

First Soldier
Boskos thromuldo boskos.

PAROLLES
I know you are the Muskos' regiment:
And I shall lose my life for want of language;
If there be here German, or Dane, low Dutch,
Italian, or French, let him speak to me; I'll
Discover that which shall undo the Florentine.

First Soldier
Boskos vauvado: I understand thee, and can speak
thy tongue. Kerely bonto, sir, betake thee to thy
faith, for seventeen poniards are at thy bosom.

PAROLLES
O!

First Soldier
O, pray, pray, pray! Manka revania dulche.

Second Lord
Oscorbidulchos volivorco.

First Soldier
The general is content to spare thee yet;
And, hoodwink'd as thou art, will lead thee on
To gather from thee: haply thou mayst inform
Something to save thy life.

PAROLLES
O, let me live!
And all the secrets of our camp I'll show,
Their force, their purposes; nay, I'll speak that
Which you will wonder at.

Cargo, cargo, cargo, villiando par corbo,
cargo.

Mercy, mercy! Do not cover my eyes.

Boskos thromuldo boskos.

I know you are the Russian regiment:
and I shall be killed for not knowing the
language; if there are any Germans, Danes, low
Dutch, Italians, or French here, let them speak
to me; I'll unfurl secrets which will let you beat
the Florentines.

Boskos vauvado: I understand you, and can
speak
your language. Kerely bonto, sir, make your
peace with God, for there are seventeen daggers
pointing at your chest.

Oh!

Pray, pray, pray!Manka revania dulche.

Oscorbidulchos volivorco.

The general is happy to spare your life for now;
and, blindfolded as you are, will take you away
for interrogation: perhaps you can tell us
something which will save your life.

O, let me live!
I'll tell you all the secrets of our camp,
their numbers, their plans; I'll tell you things
which will amaze you.

But wilt thou faithfully?

PAROLLES
If I do not, damn me.

First Soldier
Acordo linta.
Come on; thou art granted space.

Exit, with PAROLLES guarded. A short alarum within

Second Lord
Go, tell the Count Rousillon, and my brother,
We have caught the woodcock, and will keep him muffled
Till we do hear from them.

Second Soldier
Captain, I will.

Second Lord
A' will betray us all unto ourselves:
Inform on that.

Second Soldier
So I will, sir.

Second Lord
Till then I'll keep him dark and safely lock'd.

Exeunt

But will you tell us the truth?

If I don't, may I be dammed.

Acordo linta.
Come on; you have a breathing space.

Go and tell Count Rousillon, and my brother, that the bird is trapped, and we will keep him quiet until we hear from them.

Captain, I will.

He will betray us to ourselves: tell them that.

I'll do that, sir.

Until then I'll keep him in the dark and safely locked up.

SCENE II. Florence. The Widow's house.

Enter BERTRAM and DIANA

BERTRAM
They told me that your name was Fontibell.

They told me that your name was Fontibell.

DIANA
No, my good lord, Diana.

No, my good lord, Diana.

BERTRAM
Titled goddess;
And worth it, with addition! But, fair soul,
In your fine frame hath love no quality?
If quick fire of youth light not your mind,
You are no maiden, but a monument:
When you are dead, you should be such a one
As you are now, for you are cold and stern;
And now you should be as your mother was
When your sweet self was got.

*The name of the goddess;
and worthy of it, and more! But, fair soul,
is there no place for love in your fine body?
If your mind is not lit up with the heat of youth,
you are not a maiden, but a monument:
the time to be like you are now is when
you are dead, to be this cold and stern;
now you should be the same as your mother was
when you were conceived.*

DIANA
She then was honest.

She was married then.

BERTRAM
So should you be.

And you should be the same.

DIANA
No:
My mother did but duty; such, my lord,
As you owe to your wife.

*No:
my mother was just doing her duty; the same
duty, my lord, that you should do to your wife.*

BERTRAM
No more o' that;
I prithee, do not strive against my vows:
I was compell'd to her; but I love thee
By love's own sweet constraint, and will for ever
Do thee all rights of service.

*That's enough of that;
please, don't make me go against what I have
sworn on; I was forced to marry her; but I love
you with a love that is true, and will always
give you all the duties of a lover.*

DIANA
Ay, so you serve us
Till we serve you; but when you have our roses,
You barely leave our thorns to prick ourselves
And mock us with our bareness.

*Yes, that's what you say
until we give you what you want; but when you
have taken our roses, you hardly leave the
thorns for us to prick ourselves on
and you mock our exposure.*

BERTRAM
How have I sworn!

But I have sworn!

DIANA
'Tis not the many oaths that makes the truth,
But the plain single vow that is vow'd true.
What is not holy, that we swear not by,
But take the High'st to witness: then, pray you,
tell me,
If I should swear by God's great attributes,
I loved you dearly, would you believe my oaths,
When I did love you ill? This has no holding,
To swear by him whom I protest to love,
That I will work against him: therefore your
oaths
Are words and poor conditions, but unseal'd,
At least in my opinion.

It's not the quantity of promises that make the
truth, but a plain single promise that you
promise to keep.
We do not swear by things that are not wholly,
but ask God to witness them: so please, tell me,
if I swore by all God's goodness
that I loved you dearly, would you believe my
oaths, when I treated you badly? There is no
validity in swearing by the God I say I love,
to do things against his law: so your oaths
are just words and empty promises, completely
invalid,
at least in my opinion.

BERTRAM
Change it, change it;
Be not so holy-cruel: love is holy;
And my integrity ne'er knew the crafts
That you do charge men with. Stand no more
off,
But give thyself unto my sick desires,
Who then recover: say thou art mine, and ever
My love as it begins shall so persever.

Change it, change it,
don't be so piously cruel: love is holy;
and my honor has never used the tricks
which you accuse men of. Hold back no longer,
but give in to my love sickness,
and cure me: say you are mine and my love
will always go on as it started.

DIANA
I see that men make ropes in such a scarre
That we'll forsake ourselves. Give me that ring.

I see that men make ropes for their traps, hoping
that we will throw ourselves in. Give me that
ring.

BERTRAM
I'll lend it thee, my dear; but have no power
To give it from me.

I'll lend it to you, my dear, but I have no right
to give it away.

DIANA
Will you not, my lord?

You won't do it, my lord?

BERTRAM
It is an honour 'longing to our house,
Bequeathed down from many ancestors;
Which were the greatest obloquy i' the world
In me to lose.

It is an heirloom of our family,
handed down through many generations;
it would be the worst disgrace in the world
for me to lose it.

DIANA

Mine honour's such a ring:
My chastity's the jewel of our house,
Bequeathed down from many ancestors;
Which were the greatest obloquy i' the world
In me to lose: thus your own proper wisdom
Brings in the champion Honour on my part,
Against your vain assault.

My honor is a ring like that:
my chastity is the jewel of our house,
handed down through many generations;
it would be the greatest disgrace in the world
for me to lose it: so your own true words
have summoned up honor to come and defend
me against your vain attack.

BERTRAM

Here, take my ring:
My house, mine honour, yea, my life, be thine,
And I'll be bid by thee.

Here, take my ring:
my family, my honor, yes and my life, are all
yours, and I'm at your orders.

DIANA

When midnight comes, knock at my chamber-
window:
I'll order take my mother shall not hear.
Now will I charge you in the band of truth,
When you have conquer'd my yet maiden bed,
Remain there but an hour, nor speak to me:
My reasons are most strong; and you shall know
them
When back again this ring shall be deliver'd:
And on your finger in the night I'll put
Another ring, that what in time proceeds
May token to the future our past deeds.
Adieu, till then; then, fail not. You have won
A wife of me, though there my hope be done.

Come and knock on my bedroom window at
midnight:
I'll take precautions to make sure my mother
cannot hear. Now you must promise me you will
do this: when you have triumphed in my virgin's
bed, you must only stay there an hour, and you
must not speak to me: I have the strongest
reasons for this; and you will know them
when this ring is given back to you: I'll put
another ring on your finger in the night, that in
the fullness of time might show our past deeds in
the future. Goodbye, until then; do not fail then.
You have persuaded me to act like a wife, even
though doing so means I will never be one.

BERTRAM

A heaven on earth I have won by wooing thee.

Persuading you has given me a heaven on earth.

Exit

DIANA

For which live long to thank both heaven and
me!
You may so in the end.
My mother told me just how he would woo,
As if she sat in 's heart; she says all men
Have the like oaths: he had sworn to marry me
When his wife's dead; therefore I'll lie with him
When I am buried. Since Frenchmen are so
braid,
Marry that will, I live and die a maid:

And may you live long to thank both heaven and
me!
You may do so in the end.
My mother told me exactly what he would say,
as if she could see into his heart; she says all
men say the same things: he swore that he
would marry me when his wife's dead; the only
place I'll sleep with him will be the grave. Since
Frenchmen are so deceitful, let those who want
to get married, I will live and die a virgin:

Only in this disguise I think't no sin
To cozen him that would unjustly win.

Exit

but I don't think it's wrong to use these tricks to deceive the one who is trying to win something he shouldn't.

SCENE III. The Florentine camp.

Enter the two French Lords and some two or three Soldiers

First Lord
You have not given him his mother's letter?

Second Lord
I have delivered it an hour since: there is
something in't that stings his nature; for on the
reading it he changed almost into another man.

First Lord
He has much worthy blame laid upon him for
shaking
off so good a wife and so sweet a lady.

Second Lord
Especially he hath incurred the everlasting
displeasure of the king, who had even tuned his
bounty to sing happiness to him. I will tell you a
thing, but you shall let it dwell darkly with you.

First Lord
When you have spoken it, 'tis dead, and I am the
grave of it.

Second Lord
He hath perverted a young gentlewoman here in
Florence, of a most chaste renown; and this
night he
fleshes his will in the spoil of her honour: he
hath
given her his monumental ring, and thinks
himself
made in the unchaste composition.

First Lord
Now, God delay our rebellion! as we are
ourselves,
what things are we!

Second Lord
Merely our own traitors. And as in the common
course

Haven't you given him his mother's letter?

*I delivered it an hour ago: there is
something in it that really hurt him; when he
read it he became almost a different person.*

*He is much criticised, and rightly so, for
rejecting
such a good wife and such a sweet lady.*

*Especially as he has incurred the everlasting
annoyance of the King, who was ready to
provide for his happiness. I will tell you
something, but keep it under your hat.*

Whatever you say will go no further.

*He has twisted a young gentlewoman here in
Florence, who has a very chaste reputation; and
tonight
his wishes will become flesh when he takes her
virginity: he has
given her his family ring, and thinks that he has
got a good deal in exchange.*

*May God stop us from rebelling! What creatures
human beings are!*

*We are traitors to ourselves. And as is the case
with all*

of all treasons, we still see them reveal
themselves, till they attain to their abhorred
ends,
so he that in this action contrives against his
own
nobility, in his proper stream o'erflows himself.

First Lord
Is it not meant damnable in us, to be trumpeters
of
our unlawful intents? We shall not then have his
company to-night?

Second Lord
Not till after midnight; for he is dieted to his
hour.

First Lord
That approaches apace; I would gladly have him
see
his company anatomized, that he might take a
measure
of his own judgments, wherein so curiously he
had
set this counterfeit.

Second Lord
We will not meddle with him till he come; for
his
presence must be the whip of the other.

First Lord
In the mean time, what hear you of these wars?

Second Lord
I hear there is an overture of peace.

First Lord
Nay, I assure you, a peace concluded.

Second Lord
What will Count Rousillon do then? will he
travel
higher, or return again into France?

*treason, we still see them showing
themselves, until they achieve their vile purpose,
so that in his action he goes against his own
nobility, and swamps his good character.*

*Isn't it designated a sin, to boast of
our unlawful plans? So he won't be with us
tonight?*

Not until after midnight; he'll stick to his date.

*That is coming on quickly; I would have liked
him to see
his companion examined, so that he could think
about
the validity of his judgment, which made him
place such value
on this fake.*

*We won't start the business until he comes; his
presence is needed for the punishment.*

*In the meantime, what have you heard about the
war?*

I hear moves have been made for peace.

No, I can assure you peace has been agreed.

*What will Count Rousillon do then? Will he
carry on with his travels, or go back to France?*

First Lord

I perceive, by this demand, you are not altogether
of his council.

Second Lord

Let it be forbid, sir; so should I be a great deal
of his act.

First Lord

Sir, his wife some two months since fled from his
house: her pretence is a pilgrimage to Saint Jaques
le Grand; which holy undertaking with most austere
sanctimony she accomplished; and, there residing, the
tenderness of her nature became as a prey to her
grief; in fine, made a groan of her last breath, and
now she sings in heaven.

Second Lord

How is this justified?

First Lord

The stronger part of it by her own letters, which
makes her story true, even to the point of her
death: her death itself, which could not be her
office to say is come, was faithfully confirmed by
the rector of the place.

Second Lord

Hath the count all this intelligence?

First Lord

Ay, and the particular confirmations, point from
point, so to the full arming of the verity.

Second Lord

I am heartily sorry that he'll be glad of this.

First Lord

How mightily sometimes we make us comforts

*I see from your question that you are not quite
in his inner circle.*

*God forbid it, sir; if I was I would be an
accessory to his actions.*

*Sir, his wife left his house some two months ago:
her reason is to make a pilgrimage to great St
James;
she completed this holy task with strict devotion;
and, living there, her tender spirit fell victim to
her grief;
to sum up, her last breath was a groan, and
now she sings in heaven.*

Have you had proof of this?

*Most of it through her own letters, which
prove her story, even up to her death:
obviously she could not report her own death,
but it was confirmed by the clergyman in
charge.*

And does the count know all this?

*Yes, and all the details, in every
particular, guaranteeing the truth.*

I regret to say that he will be happy about this.

How terrible that we sometimes take comfort

of our losses!

from losses!

Second Lord
And how mightily some other times we drown our gain
in tears! The great dignity that his valour hath
here acquired for him shall at home be encountered
with a shame as ample.

And how at other times we lose our gains through sorrow!
The great honours that his bravery has won for him here shall be matched by an equal shame
at home.

First Lord
The web of our life is of a mingled yarn, good and
ill together: our virtues would be proud, if our faults whipped them not; and our crimes would despair, if they were not cherished by our virtues.

The web of our lives is made of tangled threads, good and
bad together: we would be proud of our virtue, if it wasn't for our faults; we would despair of our
crimes, if they weren't softened by our virtues.

Enter a Messenger

How now! where's your master?

Hello there! Where's your master?

Servant
He met the duke in the street, sir, of whom he hath
taken a solemn leave: his lordship will next morning for France. The duke hath offered him letters of commendations to the king.

He met the Duke in the street, sir, and has made his formal goodbye: his lordship will go France
tomorrow morning. The Duke has given him letters of commendation to the King.

Second Lord
They shall be no more than needful there, if they were more than they can commend.

I don't think they will be enough, even if they had more power than any recommendation.

First Lord
They cannot be too sweet for the king's tartness. Here's his lordship now.

They cannot be too sweet for the King's bitterness. Here's his Lordship now.

Enter BERTRAM

How now, my lord! is't not after midnight?

Hello there, my lord! Isn't it gone midnight?

BERTRAM
I have to-night dispatched sixteen businesses, a month's length a-piece, by an abstract of success:

I have dealt with sixteen matters tonight, each one of which could have taken a month; to sum up my successes:

I have congied with the duke, done my adieu with his
nearest; buried a wife, mourned for her; writ to my
lady mother I am returning; entertained my convoy;
and between these main parcels of dispatch effected
many nicer needs; the last was the greatest, but that I have not ended yet.

Second Lord
If the business be of any difficulty, and this
morning your departure hence, it requires haste of
your lordship.

BERTRAM
I mean, the business is not ended, as fearing to
hear of it hereafter. But shall we have this
dialogue between the fool and the soldier? Come,
bring forth this counterfeit module, he has deceived
me, like a double-meaning prophesier.

Second Lord
Bring him forth: has sat i' the stocks all night,
poor gallant knave.

BERTRAM
No matter: his heels have deserved it, in usurping
his spurs so long. How does he carry himself?

Second Lord
I have told your lordship already, the stocks carry
him. But to answer you as you would be understood;
he weeps like a wench that had shed her milk: he
hath confessed himself to Morgan, whom he supposes
to be a friar, from the time of his remembrance to

I have said goodbye to the Duke, bid farewell to his
intimates; buried a wife and mourned for her; written
to my mother to say I'm coming back; arranged my passage;
and in between all these main items I have dealt with
many smaller needs; the last one was the greatest, but
I have not finished with that one yet.

If the business is at all complex, with you leaving
in the morning your lordship will have to hurry.

What I mean is the business is not ended, as in
I'm afraid we'll hear more about it later. But shall we see
this discussion between the fool and the soldier? Come on,
bring out this false pattern, he has deceived me,
like a double talking prophesier.

Bring him out: he has sat in the stocks all night,
poor foppish scoundrel.

It doesn't matter: he deserved some pain in his heels,
having rejected his spurs for so long. How is his bearing?

I have already told your lordship, the stocks bear
him. But to answer the question as you meant it;
he's blabbing like a girl who's spilt her milk: he
has made a confession to Morgan, whom he imagines
is a friar, from his earliest memories to

this very instant disaster of his setting i' the
stocks: and what think you he hath confessed?

*the very moment of his being locked in the
stocks: and what do you think he has confessed?*

BERTRAM
Nothing of me, has a'?

There's nothing about me, is there?

Second Lord
His confession is taken, and it shall be read to
his
face: if your lordship be in't, as I believe you
are, you must have the patience to hear it.

*His confession has been written down, and it
will be read
to his face: if your lordship is in it, as I believe
you are, you must hear it patiently.*

**Enter PAROLLES guarded, and First
Soldier**

BERTRAM
A plague upon him! muffled! he can say nothing
of
me.

*A curse on him! Blindfolded! He mustn't say
anything
about me.*

First Lord
Hush, hush! Hoodman comes! Portotartarosa.

*Quiet, quiet! Here comes the blindfolded one!
Portotartarosa.*

First Soldier
He calls for the tortures: what will you say
without 'em?

*He is calling for the torturers: what will you say
without them?*

PAROLLES
I will confess what I know without constraint: if
ye pinch me like a pasty, I can say no more.

*I will confess everything I know without
reservation: if
you prick me like a pie I'll have no more to say.*

First Soldier
Bosko chimurcho.

Bosko chimurcho.

First Lord
Boblibindo chicurmurco.

Boblibindo chicurmurco.

First Soldier
You are a merciful general. Our general bids
you
answer to what I shall ask you out of a note.

*General, you are merciful. Our general orders
you
to answer this list of questions.*

PAROLLES
And truly, as I hope to live.

And I will do so truly, for my life.

First Soldier

[Reads] 'First demand of him how many horse the

duke is strong.' What say you to that?

'First ask him what number of cavalry the Duke has.' What do you say to that?

PAROLLES

Five or six thousand; but very weak and unserviceable: the troops are all scattered, and the commanders very poor rogues, upon my reputation

and credit and as I hope to live.

Five or six thousand; but they are very weak and
ineffective: they are scattered everywhere, and their commanders are very poor scoundrels, on my reputation
and credit and for my life.

First Soldier

Shall I set down your answer so?

Shall I write this down as your answer?

PAROLLES

Do: I'll take the sacrament on't, how and which way you will.

Do: I'll swear to it on anything holy, whatever you like.

BERTRAM

All's one to him. What a past-saving slave is this!

It's all the same to him. This scum is beyond redemption!

First Lord

You're deceived, my lord: this is Monsieur Parolles, the gallant militarist,--that was his own phrase,--that had the whole theoric of war in the knot of his scarf, and the practise in the chape of his dagger.

You're wrong, my lord: this is Monsieur Parolles, the gallant soldier–that was his own description–who had the whole theory of war tied up in his scarf, and the practice of it in the scabbard of his dagger.

Second Lord

I will never trust a man again for keeping his sword

clean. nor believe he can have every thing in him

by wearing his apparel neatly.

I will never trust a man again just because he keeps his sword
well polished, nor will I believe that he is a complete man
just because he's well-dressed.

First Soldier

Well, that's set down.

Well, we've got that down.

PAROLLES

Five or six thousand horse, I said,-- I will say true,--or thereabouts, set down, for I'll speak truth.

Five or six thousand horsemen, I said–I'll tell the truth–
write down that it's round about that number, for I'll tell the truth.

First Lord

He's very near the truth in this.

He's very close to the truth there.

BERTRAM
But I con him no thanks for't, in the nature he delivers it.

But I'll give him no credit for it, seeing as why he's saying it.

PAROLLES
Poor rogues, I pray you, say.

Please write down, 'poor rogues.'

First Soldier
Well, that's set down.

Right, that's written down.

PAROLLES
I humbly thank you, sir: a truth's a truth, the rogues are marvellous poor.

My humble thanks, sir: the truth is the truth and these scoundrels are very poor.

First Soldier
[Reads] 'Demand of him, of what strength they are
a-foot.' What say you to that?

'Ask him, how many infantry do they have.' What do you say to that?

PAROLLES
By my troth, sir, if I were to live this present hour, I will tell true. Let me see: Spurio, a hundred and fifty; Sebastian, so many; Corambus, so
many; Jaques, so many; Guiltian, Cosmo, Lodowick,
and Gratii, two hundred and fifty each; mine own
company, Chitopher, Vaumond, Bentii, two hundred and
fifty each: so that the muster-file, rotten and sound, upon my life, amounts not to fifteen thousand
poll; half of the which dare not shake snow from off
their cassocks, lest they shake themselves to pieces.

I swear sir, if this was my last hour I will tell the truth. Let me see: Spurio has a hundred and fifty; Sebastian the same; Corambus, the same;
Jaques, the same; Guiltian, Cosmo, Lodowick and Gratii all have two hundred and fifty each; my own
company, Chitopher, Vaumond, Bentii all have Two hundred and fifty each: so that the full army,
fit and unfit, I swear, comes to less than fifteen thousand
men; half of those dare not shake the snow off their cloaks
in case they shake themselves to pieces.

BERTRAM
What shall be done to him?

What shall we do with him?

First Lord

Nothing, but let him have thanks. Demand of him my
condition, and what credit I have with the duke.

First Soldier
Well, that's set down.

Reads
'You shall demand of him, whether one Captain Dumain
be i' the camp, a Frenchman; what his reputation is
with the duke; what his valour, honesty, and
expertness in wars; or whether he thinks it were not
possible, with well-weighing sums of gold, to
corrupt him to revolt.' What say you to this? what
do you know of it?

PAROLLES
I beseech you, let me answer to the particular of
the inter'gatories: demand them singly.

First Soldier
Do you know this Captain Dumain?

PAROLLES
I know him: a' was a botcher's 'prentice in Paris,
from whence he was whipped for getting the shrieve's
fool with child,--a dumb innocent, that could not
say him nay.

BERTRAM
Nay, by your leave, hold your hands; though I know
his brains are forfeit to the next tile that falls.

First Soldier
Well, is this captain in the duke of Florence's camp?

PAROLLES
Upon my knowledge, he is, and lousy.

---

*Nothing, just thank him. Ask him about me,
and what the Duke thinks of me.*

Right, that's written down.

*'You shall ask him, whether there is a Captain Dumain
in the camp, a Frenchman; what the Duke
thinks of him; tell us about his bravery, honesty and
military prowess; and say whether you think
it would be possible to bribe him to switch sides
with a good sum of gold.' What do you say to that?
What do you know about it?*

*May I ask that you let me answer these questions
exactly: ask them one at a time.*

Do you know this Captain Dumain?

*I know him: he was a tailor's apprentice in Paris,
but he was kicked out for getting a penniless retard
pregnant–a dumb innocent, who did not know how to say no.*

*No, if you can, hold back; though I know
he'll be killed at the next turn of the card.*

Well, is this captain part of the Duke of Florence's camp?

Yes I know he is, riddled with vermin.

First Lord
Nay look not so upon me; we shall hear of your lordship anon.

There's no need to laugh at me; we'll be hearing about your lordship soon.

First Soldier
What is his reputation with the duke?

What does the Duke think of him?

PAROLLES
The duke knows him for no other but a poor officer
of mine; and writ to me this other day to turn him
out o' the band: I think I have his letter in my pocket.

*All the Duke knows about him is that he is a poor officer
of mine; he wrote to me the other day telling me to throw him
out of the army: I think I have his letter in my pocket.*

First Soldier
Marry, we'll search.

All right, we'll search.

PAROLLES
In good sadness, I do not know; either it is there, or it is upon a file with the duke's other letters in my tent.

In all seriousness, I don't know; it's either there, or it's in a file with the Duke's other letters in my tent.

First Soldier
Here 'tis; here's a paper: shall I read it to you?

Here it is; here's a paper: shall I read it to you?

PAROLLES
I do not know if it be it or no.

I don't know if that's it or not.

BERTRAM
Our interpreter does it well.

Our interpreter is playing his part well.

First Lord
Excellently.

Wonderfully.

First Soldier
[Reads] 'Dian, the count's a fool, and full of gold,'--

'Diana, the count's a fool, and very rich,'--

PAROLLES
That is not the duke's letter, sir; that is an advertisement to a proper maid in Florence, one Diana, to take heed of the allurement of one Count
Rousillon, a foolish idle boy, but for all that

*That is not the Duke's letter, sir; that is some advice to a respectable girl in Florence, called
Diana, to watch out for the attractions of Count
Rousillon, a lazy foolish boy but very lustful*

very
ruttish: I pray you, sir, put it up again.

for all that: please sir, put it away again.

First Soldier
Nay, I'll read it first, by your favour.

No, I'll read it first, with your permission.

PAROLLES
My meaning in't, I protest, was very honest in the
behalf of the maid; for I knew the young count to be
a dangerous and lascivious boy, who is a whale to
virginity and devours up all the fry it finds.

I must point out that I was trying to take care of the girl; for I knew that the young count was a dangerous and horny boy, who is a glutton for virginity and gobbles up all he can find.

BERTRAM
Damnable both-sides rogue!

Damned two-faced scoundrel!

First Soldier
[Reads] 'When he swears oaths, bid him drop gold, and take it;
After he scores, he never pays the score:
Half won is match well made; match, and well make it;
He ne'er pays after-debts, take it before;
And say a soldier, Dian, told thee this,
Men are to mell with, boys are not to kiss:
For count of this, the count's a fool, I know it,
Who pays before, but not when he does owe it.
Thine, as he vowed to thee in thine ear,
PAROLLES.'

*'When he swears an oath, tell him to pay in advance;
once he's got what he wants he'll never pay for it: if you've got the money in your pocket then you'll be okay;
he never pays his debts afterwards, take payment in advance; and tell him, Diana, that a soldier told you this, that men are the ones for sex, boys aren't even worth getting:
to sum up, the count's a fool, I know it, he pays in advance, but won't settle his debts.
Yours, as I said to your face, Parolles.'*

BERTRAM
He shall be whipped through the army with this rhyme
in's forehead.

*He shall be whipped through the army with these words
written on his forehead.*

Second Lord
This is your devoted friend, sir, the manifold linguist and the armipotent soldier.

This is your devoted friend, sir, the great linguist and all conquering soldier.

BERTRAM
I could endure any thing before but a cat, and now
he's a cat to me.

I can put up with anything except cats, and now he's a cat to me.

First Soldier

I perceive, sir, by the general's looks, we shall be
fain to hang you.

I can see, sir, by the way the general is looking, that we shall have to hang you.

PAROLLES

My life, sir, in any case: not that I am afraid to die; but that, my offences being many, I would repent out the remainder of nature: let me live, sir, in a dungeon, i' the stocks, or any where, so I may live.

You have my life, sir, in any event: it's not that I'm afraid to die; but, as I have done so much wrong, I would like to spend the rest of my life repenting: let me live, sir, in a dungeon, in the stocks, or anywhere as long as I can live.

First Soldier

We'll see what may be done, so you confess freely;
therefore, once more to this Captain Dumain: you
have answered to his reputation with the duke and to
his valour: what is his honesty?

We'll see what we can do, as long as you tell us everything; so, let's return to this Captain Dumain: you have told us what the Duke thinks of him and about his valour: is he honest?

PAROLLES

He will steal, sir, an egg out of a cloister: for rapes and ravishments he parallels Nessus: he professes not keeping of oaths; in breaking 'em he
is stronger than Hercules: he will lie, sir, with such volubility, that you would think truth were a
fool: drunkenness is his best virtue, for he will be swine-drunk; and in his sleep he does little harm, save to his bed-clothes about him; but they
know his conditions and lay him in straw. I have but
little more to say, sir, of his honesty: he has every thing that an honest man should not have; what
an honest man should have, he has nothing.

Sir, he would steal an egg out of your stomach: for rape and assault he's equal to Nessus: he doesn't believe in keeping oaths; he's stronger Than Hercules in breaking them: he will lie, sir, with such skill, that you would think truth was foolish: what he's best at is drunkenness, he will get as drunk as a pig; he doesn't do much harm in his sleep, except to his bedclothes; but they know what he's like and they lay him down in straw. I have not much else to say about his honesty: he has every characteristic an honest man should not have and none of the ones he should have.

First Lord

I begin to love him for this.

I begin to love him for this.

BERTRAM

For this description of thine honesty? A pox

For describing your honesty like this? I say

upon him for me, he's more and more a cat.

damn him, for me he's more and more like a cat.

First Soldier
What say you to his expertness in war?

What do you say about his abilities as a soldier?

PAROLLES
Faith, sir, he has led the drum before the English
tragedians; to belie him, I will not, and more of
his soldiership I know not; except, in that
country
he had the honour to be the officer at a place
there
called Mile-end, to instruct for the doubling of
files: I would do the man what honour I can, but
of
this I am not certain.

*To tell you the truth, sir, he beats his own drum
louder
than a bunch of actors; I will not contradict him,
and I don't know anything else about his
soldiership,
except that in England he was an officer at a
place called Mile End, where he was a drill
instructor for civilians:
I want to speak of him as well as I can, but I
can't be sure
of this.*

First Lord
He hath out-villained villany so far, that the
rarity redeems him.

*He's such an extraordinary villain that
you can't help admiring him.*

BERTRAM
A pox on him, he's a cat still.

Damn him, he is still like a cat to me.

First Soldier
His qualities being at this poor price, I need not
to ask you if gold will corrupt him to revolt.

*As he is so talentless, I don't need to ask you
if he can be bribed to rebel with gold.*

PAROLLES
Sir, for a quart d'ecu he will sell the fee-simple
of his salvation, the inheritance of it; and cut the
entail from all remainders, and a perpetual
succession for it perpetually.

*Sir, for sixpence he would sell his own
salvation, all his chances of it and those
of all his descendants, he would sell it
for eternity.*

First Soldier
What's his brother, the other Captain Dumain?

*What's his brother like, the other Captain
Dumain?*

Second Lord
Why does he ask him of me?

Why is he asking him about me?

First Soldier
What's he?

What's he like?

PAROLLES
E'en a crow o' the same nest; not altogether so
great as the first in goodness, but greater a great

*He's a bird of a feather; not quite as
good as the first, but a good deal*

deal in evil: he excels his brother for a coward,
yet his brother is reputed one of the best that is:
in a retreat he outruns any lackey; marry, in coming
on he has the cramp.

more evil: he's a far greater coward than his brother, even though his brother is known as one of the greatest: in a retreat he runs faster than an errand boy; but in attack he moves like someone with cramp.

First Soldier
If your life be saved, will you undertake to betray
the Florentine?

If we spare your life, will you promise to betray the Florentine?

PAROLLES
Ay, and the captain of his horse, Count
Rousillon.

Yes, and the leader of his cavalry, Count Rousillon.

First Soldier
I'll whisper with the general, and know his
pleasure.

I'll confer with the general, and find out what he wants.

PAROLLES
[Aside] I'll no more drumming; a plague of all
drums! Only to seem to deserve well, and to
beguile the supposition of that lascivious young boy
the count, have I run into this danger. Yet who
would have suspected an ambush where I was
taken?

No more drumming for me; damnation to all drums! Just to get myself a good reputation, and to calm the suspicions of that horny young boy the count, I have got myself into this danger. Yet who would have suspected an ambush at the place they got me?

First Soldier
There is no remedy, sir, but you must die: the
general says, you that have so traitorously
discovered the secrets of your army and made such
pestiferous reports of men very nobly held, can
serve the world for no honest use; therefore you
must die. Come, headsman, off with his head.

There's nothing for it, sir, you must die: the general says that you have so treacherously given away the secrets of your army and made such scandalous reports of men who are thought to be very noble that you cannot be of any honest use to the world; so you must die. Come on, executioner, off with his head.

PAROLLES
O Lord, sir, let me live, or let me see my death!

Oh Lord, sir, let me live, or at least let me face my death!

First Lord
That shall you, and take your leave of all your
friends.

You shall do that, and say goodbye to all your friends.

Unblinding him

So, look about you: know you any here?

BERTRAM
Good morrow, noble captain.

Second Lord
God bless you, Captain Parolles.

First Lord
God save you, noble captain.

Second Lord
Captain, what greeting will you to my Lord
Lafeu?
I am for France.

First Lord
Good captain, will you give me a copy of the
sonnet
you writ to Diana in behalf of the Count
Rousillon?
an I were not a very coward, I'd compel it of
you:
but fare you well.

Exeunt BERTRAM and Lords

First Soldier
You are undone, captain, all but your scarf; that
has a knot on't yet.

PAROLLES
Who cannot be crushed with a plot?

First Soldier
If you could find out a country where but
women were
that had received so much shame, you might
begin an
impudent nation. Fare ye well, sir; I am for
France
too: we shall speak of you there.

Exit with Soldiers ?

PAROLLES

*So, have a look round: do you know anybody
here?*

Good day, noble captain.

God bless you, Captain Parolles.

God save you, noble captain

*Captain, what greeting shall I take for you to my
Lord Lafeu?
I'm off to France.*

*Good captain, will you give me a copy of the
sonnet
you wrote to Diana on behalf of Count
Rousillon?
If I wasn't a terrible coward, I'd force you to
give it to me:
but farewell.*

*You are undone, captain, everything except your
scarf; that
still has a knot in it.*

Who cannot be caught out by a plot?

*If you could discover a country where the
women
had been as shamed as you, you might begin a
cheeky nation. Goodbye, sir; I'm going to
France
as well: we shall speak of you there.*

Yet am I thankful: if my heart were great,
'Twould burst at this. Captain I'll be no more;
But I will eat and drink, and sleep as soft
As captain shall: simply the thing I am
Shall make me live. Who knows himself a braggart,
Let him fear this, for it will come to pass
that every braggart shall be found an ass.
Rust, sword! cool, blushes! and, Parolles, live
Safest in shame! being fool'd, by foolery thrive!
There's place and means for every man alive.
I'll after them.

Exit

Yet I am grateful: if I was truly good,
I'd die of shame. I will no longer be a captain;
but I'll have food and drink, and sleep as easily
as a captain: being what I am
is what will keep me alive. If you know you're a show off,
then fear this, for it will always happen
that a show off will be shown to be an ass.
Rust, sword! Cool down, blushes! And, Parolles,
live safest in shame! You have been fooled, so
profit from foolery! There's a place and a living
for every man on Earth.
I'll follow them.

122

SCENE IV. Florence. The Widow's house.

Enter HELENA, Widow, and DIANA

HELENA

That you may well perceive I have not wrong'd
you,
One of the greatest in the Christian world
Shall be my surety; 'fore whose throne 'tis
needful,
Ere I can perfect mine intents, to kneel:
Time was, I did him a desired office,
Dear almost as his life; which gratitude
Through flinty Tartar's bosom would peep forth,
And answer, thanks: I duly am inform'd
His grace is at Marseilles; to which place
We have convenient convoy. You must know
I am supposed dead: the army breaking,
My husband hies him home; where, heaven
aiding,
And by the leave of my good lord the king,
We'll be before our welcome.

So that you can see I won't do you any harm,
one of the greatest men in Christendom
will vouch for me; before I can bring my plans
to fruition
I will have to kneel before his throne:
once upon a time I did him a favour he asked,
which was almost as important to him as his
life; even a coldhearted Tatar would have been
grateful, and said thank you: I have been told
that his Grace is at Marseilles; we have
a good escort to take us there. You must know
that I'm thought to be dead: as the army is
breaking up my husband is going home; with the
help of heaven
and with the permission of my good lord the
King,
we'll get there ahead of him.

Widow

Gentle madam,
You never had a servant to whose trust
Your business was more welcome.

Gentle madam,
you never had a servant so pleased
to carry out your orders.

HELENA

Nor you, mistress,
Ever a friend whose thoughts more truly labour
To recompense your love: doubt not but heaven
Hath brought me up to be your daughter's
dower,
As it hath fated her to be my motive
And helper to a husband. But, O strange men!
That can such sweet use make of what they hate,
When saucy trusting of the cozen'd thoughts
Defiles the pitchy night: so lust doth play
With what it loathes for that which is away.
But more of this hereafter. You, Diana,
Under my poor instructions yet must suffer
Something in my behalf.

Nor have you, mistress,
ever had a friend who has thought harder about
how to repay your love: do not doubt that
heaven intended me to provide your daughter's
dowry,
just as it intended her to help me
to get myself a husband. But how strange men
are! They will have such a good time with
someone they hate when it comes to the secret
pleasures of the night:
in lust they'll play with someone they loathe,
thinking it someone else.
But more on this later. You, Diana,
under my poor orders must still suffer
something on my behalf.

DIANA

Let death and honesty
Go with your impositions, I am yours
Upon your will to suffer.

HELENA
Yet, I pray you:
But with the word the time will bring on
summer,
When briers shall have leaves as well as thorns,
And be as sweet as sharp. We must away;
Our wagon is prepared, and time revives us:
All's well that ends well; still the fine's the
crown;
Whate'er the course, the end is the renown.

Exeunt

*Even if it meant death, as long as I remain
chaste,
to follow your orders, I am yours,
and will suffer if you desire it.*

*Just wait, I ask you:
in time summer will come,
when the brambles will have leaves as well as
thorns,
and have fruit as well as pricks. We must go;
the wagon is ready, and we will get better in
time:
all's well that ends well; the prize is great;
however we get there, success will be our
reward.*

SCENE V. Rousillon. The COUNT's palace.

Enter COUNTESS, LAFEU, and Clown

LAFEU

No, no, no, your son was misled with a snipt-taffeta
fellow there, whose villanous saffron would have
made all the unbaked and doughy youth of a nation in
his colour: your daughter-in-law had been alive at
this hour, and your son here at home, more advanced
by the king than by that red-tailed humble-bee I speak of.

No, no, no, your son was led astray by a flashily dressed
fellow there, whose flamboyant ways would try
to make all the innocent youth of a nation
be like him: if your daughter-in-law was alive
now, and your son here at home, the King
would have done far better for him than that
buzzing insect I speak of.

COUNTESS

I would I had not known him; it was the death of the
most virtuous gentlewoman that ever nature had
praise for creating. If she had partaken of my
flesh, and cost me the dearest groans of a mother, I
could not have owed her a more rooted love.

I wish I had never known him; he meant death to the
most virtuous gentlewoman that nature was ever
praised for creating. If she had been born from my
womb, and given me all the pains of childbirth, I
could not have loved her more.

LAFEU

'Twas a good lady, 'twas a good lady: we may pick a
thousand salads ere we light on such another herb.

She was a good lady, a good lady: we could pick
a thousand leaves before we found another herb
like her.

Clown

Indeed, sir, she was the sweet marjoram of the
salad, or rather, the herb of grace.

Indeed, sir, she was like sweet marjoram in
a salad, or rather she was like rue.

LAFEU

They are not herbs, you knave; they are nose-herbs.

They are not for eating, you fool, they are for
perfumes.

Clown

I am no great Nebuchadnezzar, sir; I have not much
skill in grass.

I'm no great gardener, sir; I'm no good
with plants.

LAFEU
Whether dost thou profess thyself, a knave or a fool?

What do you call yourself, a knave or a fool?

Clown
A fool, sir, at a woman's service, and a knave at a man's.

When I serve a woman, sir, I am a fool, when I serve a man I am a knave.

LAFEU
Your distinction?

And what's the difference?

Clown
I would cozen the man of his wife and do his service.

I could cheat a man out of his wife and be doing him a service.

LAFEU
So you were a knave at his service, indeed.

So you would indeed be a knave in his service.

Clown
And I would give his wife my bauble, sir, to do her service.

And I would give his wife my truncheon, sir, for her service.

LAFEU
I will subscribe for thee, thou art both knave and fool.

I will bear witness for you, that you are both a knave and a fool.

Clown
At your service.

At your service.

LAFEU
No, no, no.

No thank you!

Clown
Why, sir, if I cannot serve you, I can serve as great a prince as you are.

Well sir, if I can't serve you, I can serve a prince as great as you.

LAFEU
Who's that? a Frenchman?

Who's that? A Frenchman?

Clown
Faith, sir, a' has an English name; but his fisnomy
is more hotter in France than there.

Well sir, he has an English name; but his face is redder in France than there.

LAFEU

What prince is that?

Clown
The black prince, sir; alias, the prince of
darkness; alias, the devil.

LAFEU
Hold thee, there's my purse: I give thee not this
to suggest thee from thy master thou talkest of;
serve him still.

Clown
I am a woodland fellow, sir, that always loved a
great fire; and the master I speak of ever keeps a
good fire. But, sure, he is the prince of the
world; let his nobility remain in's court. I am for
the house with the narrow gate, which I take to
be
too little for pomp to enter: some that humble
themselves may; but the many will be too chill
and
tender, and they'll be for the flowery way that
leads to the broad gate and the great fire.

LAFEU
Go thy ways, I begin to be aweary of thee; and I
tell thee so before, because I would not fall out
with thee. Go thy ways: let my horses be well
looked to, without any tricks.

Clown
If I put any tricks upon 'em, sir, they shall be
jades' tricks; which are their own right by the
law of nature.

Exit

LAFEU
A shrewd knave and an unhappy.

COUNTESS
So he is. My lord that's gone made himself
much
sport out of him: by his authority he remains
here,
which he thinks is a patent for his sauciness;

Who is this Prince?

*The black prince, sir; also known as the prince
of darkness; also known as the devil.*

*Hang on, here's my purse: I don't give you this
to drag you away from the master you're talking
about;
carry on serving him.*

*I am a man of the woods, sir, and I always loved
a great fire; and the master I speak of always
keeps
a good fire. But, to be sure, he is the prince of
the world; let his mobility stay with him. I'm
going to the house with a narrow doorway,
which is too small for great ones to enter: some
may if they humble themselves; but many will be
too fond of their comfort, they'll want to go on
the flowery path
that leads to the wide gate and the great fire.*

*Go about your business, I'm beginning to get
tired of you; I'm telling you in advance, because
I don't want to fall out with you. Go about your
business: make sure my horses are well looked
after, and don't use any shortcuts or tricks.*

*If I play any tricks with them, sir, they will be
old nag's tricks; which are naturally theirs.*

A sharp knave, and a mischievous one.

*He is that. My dead husband enjoyed him very
much,
and left instructions that he should be kept on,
which he thinks gives him permission for his
cheekiness;*

and,
indeed, he has no pace, but runs where he will.

in fact he's totally out of control.

LAFEU
I like him well; 'tis not amiss. And I was about
to
tell you, since I heard of the good lady's death
and
that my lord your son was upon his return home,
I
moved the king my master to speak in the behalf
of
my daughter; which, in the minority of them
both,
his majesty, out of a self-gracious remembrance,
did
first propose: his highness hath promised me to
do
it: and, to stop up the displeasure he hath
conceived against your son, there is no fitter
matter. How does your ladyship like it?

*I like him; I don't take offence. And I was about
to tell you, since I heard about the good lady's
death
and that my lord your son was coming home, I
asked the King, my master, to speak on behalf of
my daughter; his Majesty, without being
prompted,
remembered that he had first proposed that they
should
be married when they were children; his
Highness
has promised me that he will arrange it, and
there's no better way
to remove the displeasure he feels with your son.
What does your ladyship think of the idea?*

COUNTESS
With very much content, my lord; and I wish it
happily effected.

*I'm very happy about that, my lord; and I hope
it will be done.*

LAFEU
His highness comes post from Marseilles, of as
able
body as when he numbered thirty: he will be
here
to-morrow, or I am deceived by him that in such
intelligence hath seldom failed.

*His Highness is coming by stages from
Marseilles, as healthy
as when he was thirty years old: he will be here
tomorrow, unless I have been misinformed by
a very reliable source.*

COUNTESS
It rejoices me, that I hope I shall see him ere I
die. I have letters that my son will be here
to-night: I shall beseech your lordship to remain
with me till they meet together.

*I'm happy that I will have a chance to see him
before I die. I have had letters saying that my
son will be here
tonight: I beg your lordship to stay with me
until they meet.*

LAFEU
Madam, I was thinking with what manners I
might
safely be admitted.

*Madam, I was wondering how I could politely
ask if I could stay.*

COUNTESS

You need but plead your honourable privilege.

All you need to do is mention the privilege of your rank.

LAFEU

Lady, of that I have made a bold charter; but I thank my God it holds yet.

Lady, I've done that often enough; and I must thank God it has never let me down yet.

Re-enter Clown

Clown

O madam, yonder's my lord your son with a patch of
velvet on's face: whether there be a scar under't or no, the velvet knows; but 'tis a goodly patch of
velvet: his left cheek is a cheek of two pile and a half, but his right cheek is worn bare.

*Oh Madam, out there is my lord, your son, with a patch
of velvet on his face: whether or not there is a scar underneath it, only the velvet knows; but it is a good piece
of velvet: his left cheek has a good thick beard on it, but his right cheek is bare.*

LAFEU

A scar nobly got, or a noble scar, is a good livery
of honour; so belike is that.

A scar nobly got, or a noble scar, is a badge of honour; I expect this is.

Clown

But it is your carbonadoed face.

But it is a boiled face.

LAFEU

Let us go see your son, I pray you: I long to talk with the young noble soldier.

Please, let us go and see your son: I'm longing to talk with the young noble soldier.

Clown

Faith there's a dozen of 'em, with delicate fine hats and most courteous feathers, which bow the head
and nod at every man.

Well there's a dozen of them, with delicate fine hats and lovely feathers, which bounce and nod at everyone.

Exeunt

Act 5

SCENE I. Marseilles. A street.

Enter HELENA, Widow, and DIANA, with two Attendants

HELENA
But this exceeding posting day and night
Must wear your spirits low; we cannot help it:
But since you have made the days and nights as one,
To wear your gentle limbs in my affairs,
Be bold you do so grow in my requital
As nothing can unroot you. In happy time;

*But all this travel, day and night
must be wearing you out; it can't be helped:
but since you have given up day and night
To exhaust yourself on my behalf
be assured that you are so deserving
of my reward that nothing will stop me repaying
you. In good time—*

Enter a Gentleman

This man may help me to his majesty's ear,
If he would spend his power. God save you, sir.

*This man can help me influence his Majesty,
if he is willing to. God save you sir.*

Gentleman
And you.

And you.

HELENA
Sir, I have seen you in the court of France.

Sir, I have seen you at the French court.

Gentleman
I have been sometimes there.

I have sometimes been there.

HELENA
I do presume, sir, that you are not fallen
From the report that goes upon your goodness;
And therefore, goaded with most sharp occasions,
Which lay nice manners by, I put you to
The use of your own virtues, for the which
I shall continue thankful.

*I assume, sir, that you are still just as good
as reports say you are;
and so, spurred on by very pressing need,
which means I can't stand on ceremony, I ask you
to use your virtues in my service, for which
I will always be grateful.*

Gentleman
What's your will?

What is it you want?

HELENA
That it will please you
To give this poor petition to the king,
And aid me with that store of power you have
To come into his presence.

*That you will agree
to give this poor petition to the King,
and help me with the influence you have
to get an audience with him.*

Gentleman
The king's not here.

HELENA
Not here, sir!

Gentleman
Not, indeed:
He hence removed last night and with more
haste
Than is his use.

Widow
Lord, how we lose our pains!

HELENA
All's well that ends well yet,
Though time seem so adverse and means unfit.
I do beseech you, whither is he gone?

Gentleman
Marry, as I take it, to Rousillon;
Whither I am going.

HELENA
I do beseech you, sir,
Since you are like to see the king before me,
Commend the paper to his gracious hand,
Which I presume shall render you no blame
But rather make you thank your pains for it.
I will come after you with what good speed
Our means will make us means.

Gentleman
This I'll do for you.

HELENA
And you shall find yourself to be well thank'd,
Whate'er falls more. We must to horse again.
Go, go, provide.

Exeunt

The King's not here.

Not here, sir!

*Indeed he is not:
he left here last night, more quickly
than he usually does.*

Lord, all our efforts are for nothing!

*All's well that ends well, remember,
even though time and circumstances seem
against us.
May I ask you, where has he gone?*

*Why, as far as I know, to Rousillon;
which is where I'm going.*

*I beg you, sir,
since you are likely to see the King before me,
put this petition in his gracious hand,
which I don't think will get you into any trouble,
in fact you will be glad you took the trouble.
I will come after you as fast
as our resources permit.*

I'll do this for you.

*And you will be much thanked for it,
whatever happens. We must start travelling
again.
Go, go, help us.*

SCENE II. Rousillon. Before the COUNT's palace.

Enter Clown, and PAROLLES, following

PAROLLES
Good Monsieur Lavache, give my Lord Lafeu this
letter: I have ere now, sir, been better known to
you, when I have held familiarity with fresher
clothes; but I am now, sir, muddied in fortune's
mood, and smell somewhat strong of her strong
displeasure.

*Good Monsieur Lavache, give my Lord Lafeu this
letter: in the past you have known me
when I had cleaner clothes on; but I'm now
rather trampled in the mud by Fortune
and I smell somewhat of her displeasure.*

Clown
Truly, fortune's displeasure is but sluttish, if it
smell so strongly as thou speakest of: I will
henceforth eat no fish of fortune's buttering.
Prithee, allow the wind.

*Well, Fortune's displeasure is really pretty
filthy, if it smells as bad as you: I will not eat
any fish cooked by Fortune from now on.
Would you mind standing downwind of me?*

PAROLLES
Nay, you need not to stop your nose, sir; I spake
but by a metaphor.

*No, you needn't hold your nose, sir; I was
speaking metaphorically.*

Clown
Indeed, sir, if your metaphor stink, I will stop my
nose; or against any man's metaphor. Prithee, get
thee further.

*Indeed, sir, if your metaphor stinks, I will hold
my nose; the same as against any man's
metaphor. Please,
get further away.*

PAROLLES
Pray you, sir, deliver me this paper.

Please sir, deliver this letter for me.

Clown
Foh! prithee, stand away: a paper from fortune's
close-stool to give to a nobleman! Look, here he
comes himself.

*Pah! Stand further off, please; paper from
fortune's
lavatory to give to a nobleman! Look, here he
comes himself.*

Enter LAFEU

Here is a purr of fortune's, sir, or of fortune's
cat,--but not a musk-cat,--that has fallen into the
unclean fishpond of her displeasure, and, as he
says, is muddied withal: pray you, sir, use the
carp as you may; for he looks like a poor,

*Here's a plaything of fortune's, sir, or of
fortune's cat—not a sweet smelling cat—that has
fallen into the filthy fishpond of her displeasure,
and, as he says, he has been dirtied by it:
please, sir, treat the poor fish kindly; for he*

decayed,
ingenious, foolish, rascally knave. I do pity his
distress in my similes of comfort and leave him
to
your lordship.

Exit

PAROLLES
My lord, I am a man whom fortune hath cruelly
scratched.

LAFEU
And what would you have me to do? 'Tis too
late to
pare her nails now. Wherein have you played
the
knave with fortune, that she should scratch you,
who
of herself is a good lady and would not have
knaves
thrive long under her? There's a quart d'ecu for
you: let the justices make you and fortune
friends:
I am for other business.

PAROLLES
I beseech your honour to hear me one single
word.

LAFEU
You beg a single penny more: come, you shall
ha't;
save your word.

PAROLLES
My name, my good lord, is Parolles.

LAFEU
You beg more than 'word,' then. Cox my
passion!
give me your hand. How does your drum?

PAROLLES

looks like a poor, decayed,
cunning, foolish, rascally knave. I feel sorry
for the distress he feels at my words of comfort
so I'll leave him to your lordship.

My lord, I am a man who has been cruelly
scratched by Fortune.

What do you want me to do about it? It's too late
to trim her nails now. What have you been doing
to Fortune that has made her scratch you, for
she
is a good lady and doesn't put up with knaves
for long? Here's sixpence for you:
apply to the magistrates for relief:
I've got other things to do.

I beg your honor just to let me have a word.

I know, you just want another penny: alright,
you shall have it;
don't bother with your word.

My name, my good lord, is Parolles.

You want more than a word, then. Good
heavens!
Give me your hand. How's your drum?

O my good lord, you were the first that found
me!

LAFEU
Was I, in sooth? and I was the first that lost thee.

PAROLLES
It lies in you, my lord, to bring me in some
grace,
for you did bring me out.

LAFEU
Out upon thee, knave! dost thou put upon me at
once
both the office of God and the devil? One brings
thee in grace and the other brings thee out.

Trumpets sound

The king's coming; I know by his trumpets.
Sirrah,
inquire further after me; I had talk of you last
night: though you are a fool and a knave, you
shall
eat; go to, follow.

PAROLLES
I praise God for you.

Exeunt

*Oh my good lord, you were the first one to find
me out!*

*Was I, indeed? And I was the first one to lose
you.*

*It's up to you, my lord, to show me some favor,
since you were the one who made me lose it.*

*Get lost, knave! Are you asking me to play
both God and the Devil? One brings
you grace and the other makes you lose it.*

*The King's coming; I recognise his trumpets.
Sir,
you may ask for me later; I heard talk of you
last night: although you are a fool and a knave,
you shall
eat; come on, follow me.*

I thank God for your kindness.

SCENE III. Rousillon. The COUNT's palace.

Flourish. Enter KING, COUNTESS, LAFEU, the two French Lords, with Attendants

KING
We lost a jewel of her; and our esteem
Was made much poorer by it: but your son,
As mad in folly, lack'd the sense to know
Her estimation home.

*We lost a jewel in her, and our wealth
was greatly reduced because of it: but your son,
completely madly, didn't have the sense to know
her true worth.*

COUNTESS
'Tis past, my liege;
And I beseech your majesty to make it
Natural rebellion, done i' the blaze of youth;
When oil and fire, too strong for reason's force,
O'erbears it and burns on.

*That is the past, my lord;
I beg your Majesty to see it
as a natural rebellion, caused by the hot
headedness of youth; that raging fire can be too
strong for the force of reason,
it swamps it and roars on.*

KING
My honour'd lady,
I have forgiven and forgotten all;
Though my revenges were high bent upon him,
And watch'd the time to shoot.

*My dear lady,
I have forgiven and forgotten everything;
although I did have my revenge prepared
and was waiting for a time to attack.*

LAFEU
This I must say,
But first I beg my pardon, the young lord
Did to his majesty, his mother and his lady
Offence of mighty note; but to himself
The greatest wrong of all. He lost a wife
Whose beauty did astonish the survey
Of richest eyes, whose words all ears took captive,
Whose dear perfection hearts that scorn'd to serve
Humbly call'd mistress.

*I have to say this,
asking you to excuse me, the young lord
did a great wrong to his Majesty, his mother
and his lady; but he did the greatest wrong of all
to himself. He lost a wife
whose beauty astonished the eyes of those
who have seen many beauties, whose words
captivated all listeners,
whose absolute perfection made humble
servants
out of the proudest hearts.*

KING
Praising what is lost
Makes the remembrance dear. Well, call him hither;
We are reconciled, and the first view shall kill
All repetition: let him not ask our pardon;
The nature of his great offence is dead,
And deeper than oblivion we do bury

*Praising what has been lost
renews sweet memories. Well, call him here;
we have made up, and our first meeting
will stop any mention of the past: he doesn't
have to ask for pardon;
the details of his great offence are forgotten
and we have buried the unhappy memories of it*

The incensing relics of it: let him approach,
A stranger, no offender; and inform him
So 'tis our will he should.

beyond recovery: let him come in
with a clean slate; tell him
that I invite him to do so.

Gentleman
I shall, my liege.

I shall, my lord.

Exit

KING
What says he to your daughter? have you spoke?

What has he said to your daughter? Have you
spoken to him?

LAFEU
All that he is hath reference to your highness.

He will do whatever your Highness wishes.

KING
Then shall we have a match. I have letters sent me
That set him high in fame.

In that case we shall have a marriage. I have
received letters
which speak very well of him.

Enter BERTRAM

LAFEU
He looks well on't.

He looks well.

KING
I am not a day of season,
For thou mayst see a sunshine and a hail
In me at once: but to the brightest beams
Distracted clouds give way; so stand thou forth;
The time is fair again.

I am not always one thing nor the other
you might see sunshine and hail
coming from me at the same time: but the
darkest clouds
give way to the brightest sunbeams; so come
here, good times have returned.

BERTRAM
My high-repented blames,
Dear sovereign, pardon to me.

Dear King, please forgive me
my sins, which I greatly repent.

KING
All is whole;
Not one word more of the consumed time.
Let's take the instant by the forward top;
For we are old, and on our quick'st decrees
The inaudible and noiseless foot of Time
Steals ere we can effect them. You remember
The daughter of this lord?

The matter is finished;
we will not waste another moment on it.
Let's seize the moment with both hands;
I am old, and my most urgent orders
can be snatched away by the silent
passage of time before be can be enacted. You
remember
the daughter of this lord?

BERTRAM

Admiringly, my liege, at first
I stuck my choice upon her, ere my heart
Durst make too bold a herald of my tongue
Where the impression of mine eye infixing,
Contempt his scornful perspective did lend me,
Which warp'd the line of every other favour;
Scorn'd a fair colour, or express'd it stolen;
Extended or contracted all proportions
To a most hideous object: thence it came
That she whom all men praised and whom myself,
Since I have lost, have loved, was in mine eye
The dust that did offend it.

With admiration, my lord, she was my first choice, before my heart made my tongue speak out too rashly and I began to be full of contempt which spread to everything; it rejected a fair appearance, or thought it was faked; it warped everything and made it look hideous: and so it happened with she whom all men praised; since I have lost her I have loved her - previously my sight was affected by the dust of my stupidity.

KING

Well excused:
That thou didst love her, strikes some scores away
From the great compt: but love that comes too late,
Like a remorseful pardon slowly carried,
To the great sender turns a sour offence,
Crying, 'That's good that's gone.' Our rash faults
Make trivial price of serious things we have,
Not knowing them until we know their grave:
Oft our displeasures, to ourselves unjust,
Destroy our friends and after weep their dust;
Our own love waking cries to see what's done,
While shame full late sleeps out the afternoon.
Be this sweet Helen's knell, and now forget her.
Send forth your amorous token for fair Maudlin:
The main consents are had; and here we'll stay
To see our widower's second marriage-day.

This is well explained: the fact that you loved her removes some black marks against your name: but love that comes too late, like a remorseful apology delivered slowly, causes great offence to the Almighty, who cries, 'That is good that has been wasted.' Our stupidity makes us undervalue the best things we have, and we don't know their value until they are in their graves: we often let our unfair temper ruin our friendships and then we weep when they're dead; we let love sleep while hate does its work, when she wakes she cries to see what's happened, while to our shame hatred can sleep soundly. Let this be the funeral bell for sweet Helen, and now forget her. Send out your love token to fair Maudlin: all the main characters have given consent; and will stay here to see our widower's second wedding day.

COUNTESS

Which better than the first, O dear heaven, bless!
Or, ere they meet, in me, O nature, cesse!

Which please, dear heaven, made better than the first! Or before they meet let me die!

LAFEU

Come on, my son, in whom my house's name
Must be digested, give a favour from you
To sparkle in the spirits of my daughter,
That she may quickly come.

Come on, my son, who is going to swallow up my family name, give me a token that will make my daughter's heart leap, so that she will come quickly.

BERTRAM gives a ring

By my old beard,
And every hair that's on't, Helen, that's dead,
Was a sweet creature: such a ring as this,
The last that e'er I took her at court,
I saw upon her finger.

I swear by my old beard
and every hair in it, Helen, that sweet creature
who's dead, last time I ever saw her court
she had a ring like this on her finger.

BERTRAM
Hers it was not.

It was not hers.

KING
Now, pray you, let me see it; for mine eye,
While I was speaking, oft was fasten'd to't.
This ring was mine; and, when I gave it Helen,
I bade her, if her fortunes ever stood
Necessitied to help, that by this token
I would relieve her. Had you that craft, to reave her
Of what should stead her most?

Now, please let me see it; while I was speaking
my eye was often drawn to it.
This ring belonged to me; and, when I gave it to
Helen, I told her, that if she ever
needed help, she should send me this as a signal
and I would assist her. Were you so cunning
that you could rob her
of the thing which could help her most?

BERTRAM
My gracious sovereign,
Howe'er it pleases you to take it so,
The ring was never hers.

My gracious king,
whatever you believe,
the ring never belonged to her.

COUNTESS
Son, on my life,
I have seen her wear it; and she reckon'd it
At her life's rate.

Son, I swear on my life,
that I have seen her wearing it; and she
valued it as high is life itself.

LAFEU
I am sure I saw her wear it.

I am sure I saw her wearing it.

BERTRAM
You are deceived, my lord; she never saw it:
In Florence was it from a casement thrown me,
Wrapp'd in a paper, which contain'd the name
Of her that threw it: noble she was, and thought
I stood engaged: but when I had subscribed
To mine own fortune and inform'd her fully
I could not answer in that course of honour
As she had made the overture, she ceased
In heavy satisfaction and would never
Receive the ring again.

You are mistaken, my lord; she never saw it:
it was thrown down from a top window in
Florence to me,
wrapped in a piece of paper, on which was
written the name
of the one who threw it: she was noble, and
thought I was engaged to her: but when I told
her what my position was and let her know
that I could not honourably return her affections
she sadly accepted what I said and would never
take the ring back.

KING

Plutus himself,
That knows the tinct and multiplying medicine,
Hath not in nature's mystery more science
Than I have in this ring: 'twas mine, 'twas
Helen's,
Whoever gave it you. Then, if you know
That you are well acquainted with yourself,
Confess 'twas hers, and by what rough
enforcement
You got it from her: she call'd the saints to
surety
That she would never put it from her finger,
Unless she gave it to yourself in bed,
Where you have never come, or sent it us
Upon her great disaster.

BERTRAM

She never saw it.

KING

Thou speak'st it falsely, as I love mine honour;
And makest conjectural fears to come into me
Which I would fain shut out. If it should prove
That thou art so inhuman,--'twill not prove so;--
And yet I know not: thou didst hate her deadly,
And she is dead; which nothing, but to close
Her eyes myself, could win me to believe,
More than to see this ring. Take him away.

Guards seize BERTRAM

My fore-past proofs, howe'er the matter fall,
Shall tax my fears of little vanity,
Having vainly fear'd too little. Away with him!
We'll sift this matter further.

BERTRAM

If you shall prove
This ring was ever hers, you shall as easy
Prove that I husbanded her bed in Florence,
Where yet she never was.

Exit, guarded

*The god of riches himself,
who knows how to turn base metal into gold
does not have a greater knowledge of nature's
mysteries than I have of this ring: it was mine, it
was Helen's,
whoever gave it to you. So, if you know
what is good for you, you should
admit that it was hers, and confess to whatever
rough act
you committed to get it from her: she swore by
the saints
that she would never take it off her finger,
unless she gave it to you in bed,
which never happened, or sent it to me
when she was in great trouble.*

She never saw it.

*You are lying, I swear by my honour;
you make me think of terrible things
which I would rather shut out. If it should turn
out that you are so inhuman—I hope it won't—
and yet, I don't know: you had a terrible hate for
her, and she is dead; and there is nothing apart
from having been there myself to see it which
makes me believe that
more than seeing this ring. Take him away.*

*Whatever happens this shows that my previous
suspicions were not the product of imagination,
in fact I was not imaginative enough. Take him
away! We'll investigate this further.*

*If you can prove
this ring ever belonged to her, you can just as
easily
prove that I slept with her in Florence,
where she never went.*

KING
I am wrapp'd in dismal thinkings.

I am consumed with terrible thoughts.

Enter a Gentleman

Gentleman
Gracious sovereign,
Whether I have been to blame or no, I know not:
Here's a petition from a Florentine,
Who hath for four or five removes come short
To tender it herself. I undertook it,
Vanquish'd thereto by the fair grace and speech
Of the poor supplicant, who by this I know
Is here attending: her business looks in her
With an importing visage; and she told me,
In a sweet verbal brief, it did concern
Your highness with herself.

Gracious king,
whether I have been at fault I do not know:
here's a petition from a Florentine,
who missed her chances at four or five
of your nightly stops to give it to you herself.
I promised to do it, persuaded to by the sweet
looks and speech
of the poor petitioner, whom I know
is on her way here: she looks as though
her business is important; and she told me,
in a sweet summary, that it was to do
with you and her.

KING
[Reads] Upon his many protestations to marry me
when his wife was dead, I blush to say it, he won
me. Now is the Count Rousillon a widower: his vows
are forfeited to me, and my honour's paid to him. He
stole from Florence, taking no leave, and I follow
him to his country for justice: grant it me, O
king! in you it best lies; otherwise a seducer
flourishes, and a poor maid is undone.
DIANA CAPILET.

I'm ashamed to say that I was won over
by his many promises to marry me when his wife
was dead.
Now Count Rousillon is a widower: he has taken
my honour
and he owes me his promise. He sneaked away
from Florence without saying goodbye and I
have followed him
to his own country for justice: please grant it to
me, O king!
You have the power; otherwise a seducer
flourishes,
and a poor girl is ruined.
Diana Capilet

LAFEU
I will buy me a son-in-law in a fair, and toll for
this: I'll none of him.

I'll buy myself a son-in-law at a fair, and pay the
tax on him; I won't have anything to do with
Bertram.

KING
The heavens have thought well on thee Lafeu,
To bring forth this discovery. Seek these suitors:
Go speedily and bring again the count.
I am afeard the life of Helen, lady,
Was foully snatch'd.

God has smiled on you Lafeu,
bringing this to the surface. Get these
petitioners:
hurry and bring the count back.
I'm afraid, lady, that Helen
was foully murdered.

COUNTESS

Now, justice on the doers!

Now bring the murderers to justice!

Re-enter BERTRAM, guarded

KING
I wonder, sir, sith wives are monsters to you,
And that you fly them as you swear them lordship,
Yet you desire to marry.

I wonder, sir, why you want to marry, seeing as wives are like monsters to you,
and you run away as soon as you are engaged.

Enter Widow and DIANA

What woman's that?

Who's that woman?

DIANA
I am, my lord, a wretched Florentine,
Derived from the ancient Capilet:
My suit, as I do understand, you know,
And therefore know how far I may be pitied.

I am, my lord, a wretched Florentine,
descended from the ancient Capilet family:
I understand that you know what I'm asking for,
and so you know how much I should be pitied.

Widow
I am her mother, sir, whose age and honour
Both suffer under this complaint we bring,
And both shall cease, without your remedy.

I am her mother, sir, whose old age and honour
are both suffering due to this issue,
and I will lose both without your help.

KING
Come hither, count; do you know these women?

Come here, count; do you know these women?

BERTRAM
My lord, I neither can nor will deny
But that I know them: do they charge me further?

My lord, I cannot and will not deny
knowing them: do they accuse me of anything else?

DIANA
Why do you look so strange upon your wife?

Why do you look so oddly at your wife?

BERTRAM
She's none of mine, my lord.

She is no wife of mine, my lord.

DIANA
If you shall marry,
You give away this hand, and that is mine;
You give away heaven's vows, and those are mine;
You give away myself, which is known mine;

If you marry,
you reject this hand, and that is mine;
you break heaven's vows, and those are mine;
you reject me, who we know is mine;
for I am by my vows so intertwined with you

For I by vow am so embodied yours,
That she which marries you must marry me,
Either both or none.

LAFEU
Your reputation comes too short for my
daughter; you
are no husband for her.

BERTRAM
My lord, this is a fond and desperate creature,
Whom sometime I have laugh'd with: let your
highness
Lay a more noble thought upon mine honour
Than for to think that I would sink it here.

KING
Sir, for my thoughts, you have them ill to friend
Till your deeds gain them: fairer prove your
honour
Than in my thought it lies.

DIANA
Good my lord,
Ask him upon his oath, if he does think
He had not my virginity.

KING
What say'st thou to her?

BERTRAM
She's impudent, my lord,
And was a common gamester to the camp.

DIANA
He does me wrong, my lord; if I were so,
He might have bought me at a common price:
Do not believe him. O, behold this ring,
Whose high respect and rich validity
Did lack a parallel; yet for all that
He gave it to a commoner o' the camp,
If I be one.

COUNTESS
He blushes, and 'tis hit:
Of six preceding ancestors, that gem,

*that she who marries you must marry me,
either both or none.*

*Your reputation is too low for my daughter; you
shall not marry her.*

*My lord, this is an affectionate and mad
creature,
with whom I have sometimes shared a joke: let
your Highness
think better of my honor than that I would
give it up for her.*

*Sir, as my for thoughts for they will not be
friendly toyou
until you give me some reason: show that your
honor
is better than I am imagining.*

*My good lord,
ask him to swear on oath that he
did not take my virginity.*

What have you got to say to her?

*She's cheeky, my lord,
and had plenty of men in the camp.*

*He does me wrong, my lord; if I was like that
he could have bought me a low price:
do not believe him. Look at this ring,
which cannot be matched for richness
and craftsmanship; and yet he says
he gave it to a cheap whore in the camp,
if I am one.*

*He blushes, that hit home:
Six of his forebears*

Conferr'd by testament to the sequent issue,
Hath it been owed and worn. This is his wife;
That ring's a thousand proofs.

have owned and worn that ring,
handing it down in their wills. This is his wife;
that ring proves it a thousand times over.

KING
Methought you said
You saw one here in court could witness it.

I thought you said
that someone here in the court could testify for
you.

DIANA
I did, my lord, but loath am to produce
So bad an instrument: his name's Parolles.

I did, my lord, but I hate having to use
such a bad tool: his name is Parolles.

LAFEU
I saw the man to-day, if man he be.

I saw the man today, if he is a man.

KING
Find him, and bring him hither.

Find him and bring him here.

Exit an Attendant

BERTRAM
What of him?
He's quoted for a most perfidious slave,
With all the spots o' the world tax'd and
debosh'd;
Whose nature sickens but to speak a truth.
Am I or that or this for what he'll utter,
That will speak any thing?

You're going to believe him?
He's known as a treacherous slave,
who is accused of all the debauched sins of the
world:
it would kill him to tell the truth.
It is my fate going to be decided on the evidence
of a man who will say anything?

KING
She hath that ring of yours.

She has your ring.

BERTRAM
I think she has: certain it is I liked her,
And boarded her i' the wanton way of youth:
She knew her distance and did angle for me,
Madding my eagerness with her restraint,
As all impediments in fancy's course
Are motives of more fancy; and, in fine,
Her infinite cunning, with her modern grace,
Subdued me to her rate: she got the ring;
And I had that which any inferior might
At market-price have bought.

I think she has: I certainly liked her,
and slept with her as a reckless youth will:
she knew her game and made a play for me,
leading me on by pretending to be modest,
as the harder it is to get something
the more one wants it; and, to sum up,
her great cunning, with her commonplace
beauty,
made me pay her price: she got the ring;
and I got what any lowlife might
have got at the standard rate.

DIANA

I must be patient:
You, that have turn'd off a first so noble wife,
May justly diet me. I pray you yet;
Since you lack virtue, I will lose a husband;
Send for your ring, I will return it home,
And give me mine again.

BERTRAM
I have it not.

KING
What ring was yours, I pray you?

DIANA
Sir, much like
The same upon your finger.

KING
Know you this ring? this ring was his of late.

DIANA
And this was it I gave him, being abed.

KING
The story then goes false, you threw it him
Out of a casement.

DIANA
I have spoke the truth.

Enter PAROLLES

BERTRAM
My lord, I do confess the ring was hers.

KING
You boggle shrewdly, every feather stars you.
Is this the man you speak of?

DIANA
Ay, my lord.

KING
Tell me, sirrah, but tell me true, I charge you,
Not fearing the displeasure of your master,
Which on your just proceeding I'll keep off,

I must be patient:
you, who rejected such a noble first wife,
are also cutting me off. But please;
since you lack virtue, I'll give you up as a
husband; send for your ring, I'll send it back,
and you give me back mine.

I haven't got it.

What was your ring, may I ask?

Sir, it was very like
the one on your finger.

Do you know this ring? It used to belong to him
until recently.

This was the one that I gave him in bed.

Then it's not true that you threw it down to him
from a window.

I have told the truth.

My lord, I admit the ring was hers.

You're a bit skittish, you jump at shadows.
Is this the man you spoke of?

Yes, my lord.

Tell me, sir, and I order you to tell me the truth,
without worrying about punishment from your
master, which I'll protect you from if you're

By him and by this woman here what know
you?

honest, what do you know about his relationship
with this woman?

PAROLLES
So please your majesty, my master hath been an
honourable gentleman: tricks he hath had in
him,
which gentlemen have.

If it pleases your Majesty, my master has been
an honourable gentleman: he's got up to some
tricks,
as gentlemen will.

KING
Come, come, to the purpose: did he love this
woman?

Come on, get to the point: did he love this
woman?

PAROLLES
Faith, sir, he did love her; but how?

Well yes sir, he did love her; but how did he?

KING
How, I pray you?

Well you tell me.

PAROLLES
He did love her, sir, as a gentleman loves a
woman.

He loved her, sir, as a gentleman loves a
woman.

KING
How is that?

And in what way is that?

PAROLLES
He loved her, sir, and loved her not.

He loved her, sir, and didn't love her.

KING
As thou art a knave, and no knave. What an
equivocal companion is this!

And you're a knave, and not a knave. What a
double speaking chap you are!

PAROLLES
I am a poor man, and at your majesty's
command.

I am a poor man, and at your Majesty's orders.

LAFEU
He's a good drum, my lord, but a naughty orator.

He makes a lot of noise, my lord, but not so
much sense.

DIANA
Do you know he promised me marriage?

Do you know he promised to marry me?

PAROLLES
Faith, I know more than I'll speak.

Well, I know more than I'll tell.

KING
But wilt thou not speak all thou knowest?

Won't you tell everything you know?

PAROLLES
Yes, so please your majesty. I did go between them,
as I said; but more than that, he loved her: for indeed he was mad for her, and talked of Satan and
of Limbo and of Furies and I know not what: yet I
was in that credit with them at that time that I knew of their going to bed, and of other motions,
as promising her marriage, and things which would
derive me ill will to speak of; therefore I will not speak what I know.

Yes, as your Majesty pleases, I was their go-between,
as I said; but more than that, he loved her: in fact
he was mad for her, and talked of Satan and Limbo and Furies and goodness knows what: but I
was close enough to them at the time that I knew about them sleeping together, and other offers,
which amounted to a marriage proposal, and there are other things which I would get disapproved of if I spoke about them; so I will not say what I know.

KING
Thou hast spoken all already, unless thou canst say
they are married: but thou art too fine in thy evidence; therefore stand aside.
This ring, you say, was yours?

You said it all already, unless you can say that they are now married: but your evidence is too devious; so step aside.
You say this ring was yours?

DIANA
Ay, my good lord.

Yes, my good lord.

KING
Where did you buy it? or who gave it you?

Where did you buy it? Or who gave it to you?

DIANA
It was not given me, nor I did not buy it.

It was not given to me, nor did I buy it.

KING
Who lent it you?

Who lent it to you?

DIANA
It was not lent me neither.

It wasn't lent to me either.

KING
Where did you find it, then?

Where did you find it then?

DIANA
I found it not.

I didn't find it.

KING
If it were yours by none of all these ways,
How could you give it him?

If you didn't come by it in any of these ways,
how could you give it to him?

DIANA
I never gave it him.

I never gave it to him.

LAFEU
This woman's an easy glove, my lord; she goes off
and on at pleasure.

This woman is like a loose glove, my lord; very
easy to change.

KING
This ring was mine; I gave it his first wife.

This ring used to belong to me; I gave it to his
first wife.

DIANA
It might be yours or hers, for aught I know.

It might be yours or hers, for all I know.

KING
Take her away; I do not like her now;
To prison with her: and away with him.
Unless thou tell'st me where thou hadst this ring,
Thou diest within this hour.

Take her away; I've had enough of her.
Put her in prison, and take him away too.
Unless you tell me where you got this ring from
you'll be dead within the hour.

DIANA
I'll never tell you.

I'll never tell you.

KING
Take her away.

Take her away.

DIANA
I'll put in bail, my liege.

I'll apply for bail, my lord.

KING
I think thee now some common customer.

I now think you're a common prostitute.

DIANA
By Jove, if ever I knew man, 'twas you.

I'm just as likely to have slept with you as with
any other man.

KING
Wherefore hast thou accused him all this while?

Then why have you accused him all this time?

DIANA
Because he's guilty, and he is not guilty:
He knows I am no maid, and he'll swear to't;

Because he's guilty, and he is not guilty:
he knows I'm not a virgin, and he'll swear to it;

I'll swear I am a maid, and he knows not.
Great king, I am no strumpet, by my life;
I am either maid, or else this old man's wife.

KING
She does abuse our ears: to prison with her.

DIANA
Good mother, fetch my bail. Stay, royal sir:

Exit Widow

The jeweller that owes the ring is sent for,
And he shall surety me. But for this lord,
Who hath abused me, as he knows himself,
Though yet he never harm'd me, here I quit him:
He knows himself my bed he hath defiled;
And at that time he got his wife with child:
Dead though she be, she feels her young one kick:
So there's my riddle: one that's dead is quick:
And now behold the meaning.

Re-enter Widow, with HELENA

KING
Is there no exorcist
Beguiles the truer office of mine eyes?
Is't real that I see?

HELENA
No, my good lord;
'Tis but the shadow of a wife you see,
The name and not the thing.

BERTRAM
Both, both. O, pardon!

HELENA
O my good lord, when I was like this maid,
I found you wondrous kind. There is your ring;
And, look you, here's your letter; this it says:
'When from my finger you can get this ring
And are by me with child,' & c. This is done:
Will you be mine, now you are doubly won?

I'll swear I am a virgin, and he doesn't know it.
Great King, I am no tart, I swear;
I am either a virgin or I'm married to this old man.

She's messing us about: sling her in jail.

Good mother, fetch my bondsman. Wait, your Majesty:

The jeweler that owns the ring has been sent for,
and he will surely acquit me. As for this Lord,
who has abused me, as he himself knows,
though he has never harmed me, I acquit him:
he knows that he has defiled my bed,
and at that time he got his wife pregnant.
Although she's dead, she can feel her baby kick:
there's my riddle: someone who is dead is alive:
and now see the solution.

Is there a wizard
who has tricked my eyes?
Is this real?

No, my good lord;
you see just the shadow of a wife,
in name and not in fact.

You are both, both. Forgive me!

My good lord, when you thought I was this girl
you were very kind to me. There's your ring;
and look, here's your letter; it says this:
'When you get this ring off my finger
and are pregnant by me,' etc. This has been done:
Will you be mine, now I've won you twice?

BERTRAM
If she, my liege, can make me know this clearly,
I'll love her dearly, ever, ever dearly.

My lord, if she can explain this to me,
I will love her dearly for ever.

HELENA
If it appear not plain and prove untrue,
Deadly divorce step between me and you!
O my dear mother, do I see you living?

If you can't understand and it's not true
then may we get divorced!
Oh my dear mother, are you alive?

LAFEU
Mine eyes smell onions; I shall weep anon:

My eyes feel like I've been chopping onions: I
shall cry soon.

To PAROLLES

Good Tom Drum, lend me a handkercher: so,
I thank thee: wait on me home, I'll make sport
with thee:
Let thy courtesies alone, they are scurvy ones.

Good Tom Drum, lend me a handkerchief: good,
thank you: wait for me at home, we'll have some
fun:
don't bother with your thanks, it's worthless.

KING
Let us from point to point this story know,
To make the even truth in pleasure flow.

Let me know this story from beginning to end,
let's enjoy the truth.

To DIANA

If thou be'st yet a fresh uncropped flower,
Choose thou thy husband, and I'll pay thy
dower;
For I can guess that by thy honest aid
Thou keep'st a wife herself, thyself a maid.
Of that and all the progress, more or less,
Resolvedly more leisure shall express:
All yet seems well; and if it end so meet,
The bitter past, more welcome is the sweet.

If you are in fact still a virgin,
choose yourself a husband, and I'll pay your
dowry;
I can see that with your playful help
you have given a wife back her position, and
stayed a virgin. We'll learn all about this in
good time: Everything seems to have turned out
for the best; and if it ends so well
the bitterness of the past makes this sweetness
more welcome.

Flourish
EPILOGUE

KING
The king's a beggar, now the play is done:
All is well ended, if this suit be won,
That you express content; which we will pay,
With strife to please you, day exceeding day:
Ours be your patience then, and yours our parts;
Your gentle hands lend us, and take our hearts.

The play is over, now the King is a beggar:
Everything has ended well, if we have succeeded
in pleasing you; we make our best efforts
to do this, day after day:
now it's time for you to act for us;
give us your applause, and we will be grateful.

Exeunt

Made in the USA
San Bernardino, CA
11 February 2016